GRACE UNDER PRESS

GRACE UNDER PRESSURE

& Other Stool Pigeon
Stories

Edited, with an introduction by

PHIL HEBBLETHWAITE

JUNKO PARTNERS PUBLISHING

First published in 2010 by Junko Partners Publishing,
publishers of The Stool Pigeon music newspaper.
21a Maury Road, London, N16 7BP

thestoolpigeon.co.uk

© Junko Partners Publishing, 2010

All rights reserved. No part of this publication may be reproduced, stored in a retrieval system, or
transmitted, in any form or by any means, electronic, mechanical, photocopying, recording, or
otherwise, without the prior permission of the publisher.

ISBN: 978-0-9565246-1-4

Typeset in Fournier by Mickey Gibbons
Printed and bound by Short Run Press, Exeter, Devon

CONTENTS

——————————— ★ ———————————

INTRODUCTION
By Phil Hebblethwaite,
Editor of The Stool Pigeon

What follows is a collection of our attempts to try and do something true with what everyone keeps insisting is a dying discipline — music journalism. These are stories that, hopefully, pay no attention to what record companies and PR people want from the music press and they're never signed off, here or when they were first published, with: 'The new album by _____ is out now on _____.' Plenty of them are long and lend themselves to being printed, first on newspaper and now book pages, and they don't care much about the dramatic changes in the music business since *The Stool Pigeon* has been around — 2005 to the present. Rather, they pray that things as old as the hills — writing, story-telling, reporting — can still count, even after the money for music journalism dried up and every hack in every field finds themselves a gnat's hair away from re-writing press releases for some frigging mobile phone company. And I know the whole idea of this book makes little sense in our age of mass attention deficit disorder, but we've always been the kind of idiots who will stick an extra eight pages in the paper each time someone moans that it's overwhelming.

The backbone of *Grace Under Pressure* is epic Q&As with musicians who deserve to be allowed to talk without the writer getting in the way. Of course, it's still all the writer, but the beauty's in the guidance and it often leads to dynamite. Then there are straight narratives — some built upon interviews, some just yarns — and also included are plenty of stories that went drastically wrong. They get written after a journalist calls, in despair and sometimes humiliated, to say they got *nothing* out of an interview when in fact they got everything that people actually want to read about.

I picked these 19 stories because they're my favourites and it's a

1

coincidence that most, but not all, of the hardcore *Stool Pigeon* contributors have a selection included. We're something of a motley crew made up of pro music writers, an aviation journalist, someone who normally reports on environmental issues, practising musicians, a hip hop head who now works for a CD replication company and, in the case of Memphis Pie and Tony Gunnarsson, two friends of mine who'd never been published before. I'm ashamed that only three of these selections are written by women, but I love it that everyone, even those not featured, does wildly different things outside of contributing to the paper. It helps the writing to have what I think is a unique spirit that also comes from *The Stool Pigeon* remaining passionately independent and boorishly determined to try and tell it like it is.

Some consideration was given to who these articles are about, but not much. It was never the point to compile a book based on the better-known subjects we've covered. That said, matching up a brilliant interviewer with a superstar can be exhilarating and it's no surprise that we begin with the rampantly intellectual mind of John Doran taking on Marilyn Manson. The book is also named after John's priceless interview with Grace Jones, and now that the selections are final, it's become obvious that the best music inspires the best writing. Included are pieces on many incredible bands and artists — *exactly* the kind of people we dreamed of having in the paper when we launched five years ago.

Perhaps there's something quaint about publishing a five-year anniversary *Stool Pigeon* book when the zeitgeist dictates we probably ought to have spent the time on a damn blog or something. So be it. *Grace Under Pressure* is for people like the short-sighted dude I saw reading a copy of the paper two inches in front of his face while walking in Soho a year or so ago. He tripped on a bag of rubbish, went arse over tit, then got up and carried on reading as if nothing had happened. That man has no idea that he's point number one in my argument for the continuing majesty of the printed word.

March 2010

THE DOPE SHOW

*Marilyn Manson promised us champagne and caviar, but now he's only capable of
delivering cola and crisps. He's become little more than the God of Fucking About.*

By JOHN DORAN

From issue 22, Summer 2009

Today the God of Fuck is merely the Petty Officer of Fucking About;
the Local Ombudsman of Mildly Irritating Behaviour. He's locked in
his suitably grand room at a Park Lane hotel with plenty of absinthe and
'a young lady friend'. A wide-eyed reporter from a London free title
eventually comes down the stairs declaring him to be "leathered";
saying that the lanky industro-goth was striding round his room with
the girl tossed over his shoulder, chatting bare nonsense. Seasoned
veterans of idiotic American rock star behaviour, we pack up and go
home leaving a business-like but inexperienced guy from the BBC alone
in the foyer waiting dutifully for an interview. Predictably, his copy,
when it appears online a few days later, is a riot of non-sequiturs; a
throbbing psychedelic grotto of drunken nonsense. It isn't the poor
hack's fault. Simply, Manson has become the God of Fucking Can't Be
Arsed; the Bursar of Talent Seepage; the Heir of Nothing In Particular.

A few days later, he blows out the rearranged *Stool Pigeon* interview
as well, and not only has he sacked us off, he hasn't even turned up to
his pre-tour rehearsals in Germany. "No one knows where he is," says
his PR guy. The world tour starts in 48 hours.

Of course, none of this would be remarkable if it wasn't for the sheer
weight of 'I can't be bothered' emanating from Brian Warner's seventh
long player, *The High End Of The Low*. His albums have been patchy
efforts for some time now — since 2000's *Holy Wood (In The Shadow Of
The Valley Of Death)* to be precise — and apart from the occasional
mint single ('mOBSCENE' springs to mind), Manson has made little
effort to change things. If it weren't for his distinctively battered,
schlocky and operatic brogue, some of the songs on *The High End Of*

The Low wouldn't be out of place on a Nickelback album, or a recent outing by Oasis.

The album was written after some young actress or other left him. He can't have thought much of her if this is his elegy to their relationship. He certainly doesn't think much of you, if you're still one of his fans. In fact, he must think you're a clueless and tasteless idiot.

Even Trent Reznor, his former mentor, recently called him a "dopey clown" in *Mojo* magazine: "He is a malicious guy and will step on anybody's face to succeed and cross any line of decency. Seeing him now, drugs and alcohol now rule his life and he's become a dopey clown. He used to be the smartest guy in the room. And as a fan of his talents, I hope he gets his shit together. During the [Downward] Spiral tour [in 1994-95], we propped them up to get our audience turned on to them and at that time a lot of the people in my circle were pretty far down the road as alcoholics. Not Manson. His drive for success and self-preservation was so high, he pretended to be fucked up a lot when he wasn't."

When we eventually catch up with Manson the next day, it's clear he has indeed been putting in a lot of time at the coke face; hoofing lines of chisel up his prodigious nose; belting fat slugs of Charleston straight into his nozzle until he can't hear what anyone else around him is saying. It's hard to tell from a straight transcript, but he motor-mouths, runny-nosed and sniffing, at 100mph through the interview like a long-faced jabberwocky competing in a verbal Wacky Races, either oblivious to or unconcerned with the questions that are being asked.

It wasn't always thus. After an almost painfully normal and nerdy childhood in the 1970s and 1980s, Brian Warner moulded himself into goth provocateur Marilyn Manson (a combination of the first name of an iconic beauty and the last name of a notorious killer, just as with other collaborators such as Twiggy Ramirez). He formed The Spooky Kids (the original incarnation of the act still surviving today) in 1989 influenced by industrial bands such as Ministry and Nine Inch Nails, but with a much heavier emphasis on the glam and the grotesque. In fact, they took the industrial metal blueprint and amped up both the image and the transgressive nature of the lyrics but, importantly, added a pop accessibility to the music. The combination was dynamite. He went on to sell 44 million albums worldwide and was arguably the most iconic figure in rock of the 1990s; the evil Elvis to Eminem's Sinatra.

And this is what makes his failure to climb out of his artistic slump depressing; this fallow period of the not-so naughty noughties. Because even after fighting his way through a snowstorm, he's still one of the most interesting and intelligent people this newspaper has ever had the privilege of speaking to, and his off-the-cuff gibbering would put the faux-intellectualism of most musicians to shame. The trouble is, Manson has turned out to be our generation's Alice Cooper and not our David Bowie. And you only have to talk to him for a few minutes to realise that he could still be so much more... if he had the inclination.

THE STOOL PIGEON: I want to ask you about the role of transgression in rock music, where transgression is going, and even if the outrageous, controversial rock star of the late 20th Century might be redundant.

MARILYN MANSON: I think by its nature it's redundant. You can't really ever make any art without getting someone's attention... constantly. You have to say something differently, constantly. Dali said that anyone who doesn't steal isn't an artist and you have to take things and make them your own, and then when you've done that, you have to realise how not to cannibalise yourself, but how to transform constantly. This record I've just made allows people to witness that I've made a transformation. All music comes from heartache and all music comes from pain and suffering. That's never going to go away, so how do we learn to adapt to the fact that the whole world is able to talk really loud now? You know, everyone's a journalist now — everyone's got an opinion — and I think that just levels the playing field. Andy Warhol told us that everyone would be famous for 15 minutes and he was very accurate. So we have to invent new ways to make it interesting to other people because we're trying to appeal to other people. You have to make this conversation interesting to someone else who wants to read it.

SP: One of the last things Plato wrote was, and I'm paraphrasing, 'What's got into the kids? The kids have gone fucking mental.' So that thing of fearing what the next generation is up to has always been with us. But I'm also talking about the hyper-acceleration of culture. Say, for example, if you had written a song like your new single 'Arma-Goddamn-Motherfuckin-Geddon' as the follow up to 'Lunchbox' at the start of your career, people would have found it a lot more shocking than they do now.

MM: Oh, I think it is completely unshocking and completely intentionally redundant and that was the whole point of it. I really go out of my way to make that fit into the record. In the context of the record, it refers to something I said that day going to the studio. It was my commentary on how shameless and hopeless and uninteresting things are now. When you have to put 'goddamn' and 'motherfucking' into a title that already has 'Armageddon' in it... you know! I was just making a point. Anyway, I didn't write it — the *Bible* wrote it — I just added a couple of new words to it. If it were Scrabble and I just threw the letters down and they came up that way, would it be my fault that they ended up in that sequence? [laughs] Not really. I just pushed the button. Cue applause. And people clapped. Canned laughter. You know what the worst thing about canned laughter is? That everyone on the tapes for canned laughter is dead now. So it's a room full of dead people laughing at me.

SP: What is the primary role of the transgressive rock star? Is it to provide a safe space for kids to rebel in? Is it to hold up a mirror to society?

MM: No, it's for girls. It's so you can get girls. Perhaps not everyone should be simplified in rock'n'roll or art. It's not a girl in everyone's case. But I think the only reason anyone makes anything is because they want to connect with somebody. And I think with rock'n'roll it comes down to being a rock star. It's not oversimplifying what I do to say that; it would be simplifying the reason why I do it. I've said it right from the beginning: that I wanted to share the same feeling that I think everybody has. And I wanted to be a rock star because you get away with doing and saying things and not having to do other things. You sidestep the thing you see in front of you — this horrible future of 9-to-5; slavery dressed up in the form of a pay cheque. Right now if I had to do something else, or if I was not able to do what I do, I don't think there would be a point. That's not being cynical — it's just that I've seen so much. I couldn't work like an everyday person. I think I work harder than anyone I know — it's just that sometimes my work is doing drugs, drinking and taking my pants off in front of girls. Sometimes it's writing words that get me to the point where I can take my pants off in front of girls; sometimes it's writing a melody; sometimes it's getting back together with my best friend [Twiggy Ramirez] and taking his pants off while he is playing guitar.

SP: Was there much mutual uncloaking of trouser regions going on between you and Twiggy now that you're making music together again?

MM: [laughs] Well, I think there was, really. I made that comment metaphorically, but I guess I've spent 10 years saying, 'Why can't we find the right guitarist to play the guitar parts that Twiggy wrote?' And it was right there in front of my face. The guitar is like the microphone and it has to be played with... feeling. Sometimes you play from your dick and sometimes you play from your heart, but not from your wallet or not from your head. It has to be instinctual. The stuff that he played on this record was how I felt inside. We were going through the same things emotionally, even though you can never compare these things. I never say to someone, 'Oh, I know how you feel.' You never know how someone feels. I write a song and say, 'This is how I feel.' And if people can relate to it, they can put themselves into it.

SP: You're known, in the terms of American rock and alternative music, as the most far-out person going. You're the God of Fuck...

MM: I did like it when the *NME*... and the *NME* have shat upon some of the greatest artists. I saw an anniversary issue where they said

'Diamond Dogs: The End of Bowie'... So they called me the God of Fuck-All and I liked that. I thought that was pretty good.

SP: It's not even a dis to you, is it? It's a bald statement of nihilism...

MM: No, I think it's pretty funny. I think it's pretty funny because it's someone not realising that you can't be me without having a pretty good sense of humour. That's the point. My name's Marilyn Manson. People think I'm going to come across all serious. Do I have to go to work and be all serious and be aggressive and the God of Fuck and whatever? I have to laugh about it, really.

SP: This is relatively serious: I was thinking about the fall of Rome. Contrary to this idea of wailing and gnashing of teeth, the overall theme was one of boredom. If you're Public Enemy Number 1 of American society — which you are to some, I guess — what happens when people become bored of you? What happens when people aren't shocked by you anymore?

MM: Well, I think journalism is in a sad state when I know that it is the proper thing to say that Marilyn Manson is not shocking. It's been like that from the beginning; it's never been proper to say that I'm shocking. Jane's Addiction recorded one of the most influential records in my life, *Nothing's Shocking*. Were we ever shocked as kids? No, we were fascinated. When in Rome, get a Caesarean section. They invented that, you know. On this album, I feel like I can hear myself when I listen back to it, almost becoming Nero at the end of it and saying, 'You know what? If I can't have love I'll burn everything down.' But that is a cliché. I think this record is about the fact that we all give up something because we want to have the thing we cannot have. And for most of us it's always love or someone to understand us — not to fit in, but it is to fit in. People try and fit into a pair of jeans — fit in with the crowd. Some people try to fit into a porn star. And it's trying to connect. Someone always gives up their wings to be mortal — to try and obtain that unobtainable thing. But it's when you give up the wings... that's when

8

you don't get it. So I have to be reminded the hard way that I was the person who spent the later part of my earlier life saying, 'Don't be afraid to be yourself.' And I think I started being afraid of being myself because I was worried that being myself wasn't what I should be any more, because, as a person who is so critical of everything, being me wasn't going to be interesting enough anymore. I had to just let go. Do you know what I mean?

SP: No.

MM: A kid shot his teacher last week and said, 'Hail Marilyn Manson.' If that keeps on happening and I keep getting blamed for it… and I suppose I should be blamed for something if my name is included in a sentence that ends with a bullet instead of a full stop. But is it my fault? Is it the world's fault? Whose fault is it? I don't know. Is anyone else saying my name?

SP: Well…

MM: Is anyone else saying my name and shooting people? Or are people saying, 'I believe in Jesus Christ.' Bang! 'I believe in Islam.' Bam! 'I believe in America.' Boom!

SP: But that's not…

MM: So it is sadly impressive that something like that happens. But, at the same time, as a critic of the world, I think it doesn't really matter what I say or do anymore. Apparently it does, though. Maybe it matters in the wrong way sometimes, but I don't think I'm being irresponsible.

SP: Rewind for a second. I've read about the case that you're talking about. [Fifteen-year-old Justin Doucet who, during a recent tooled-up rampage, managed to kill no one, despite shooting at his teacher at point-blank range and then himself in the head.] Doesn't the blame for this lie squarely at the feet of those opposing change to gun law? Doesn't the blame lie with the gun industry in the United States?

MM: Mmmm. You could, I guess, start with that, but do you think that kid would have stopped with that train of thought just because he couldn't get a gun?

SP: Of course he would have!

MM: That if there wasn't a gun, he wouldn't have done it with a pencil? I don't mean writing! Obviously it would have been great if he had done the same thing with a pencil! Which is fortunately what I chose to do, if we're speaking in broad brushstrokes and metaphors. There is a very fine line between artists and killers. That's what separates art from commerce. Art and spirituality go hand in hand. But politics and religion are not spiritual — they take things out of the world. That's not to say that you can't believe in God. For me, God is the concept of making something. If you don't have hope for the future, then you can't be an artist — there's no point. Everyone thinks I'm a nihilist or a fatalist and I came dangerously close to thinking like that over the past few years. It was when I started to think that I don't have any feelings any more, so why bother? That is the end. Boredom. Boredom leads to drugs. Boredom leads to, 'Let's invent new things because we've done them all.' It's funny that you bring up the Roman Empire because the kids have always been too cynical and grown up too fast. Kids are senile now. They forget. They have no history. It's Twitter, Twitter, download, download. I don't care about any of that. What are you saying? What do you have to say? Can you say something? Can you say something that is passionate? And sometimes, yeah, do I want to shoot some of these people? Sure. You should be worried about what I'd do, if you're worried about what my music does. There's gonna be a day when I shoot someone and it's gonna be myself or someone who says the wrong thing to me and I'm not afraid to do it. I don't want to go to jail and right now I don't want to die, so you have to make that choice. Are you stupid or are you passionate? Pick between the two. And sadly, when kids go wild, it's stupid. 'When Kids Go Wild!' It's a new TV show and they're going to put my music on the soundtrack!

SP: I genuinely think kids from pretty much any country in the world would go mad and kill people if they were allowed to. And by allowed to, I mean if there were guns in the family home or local shop that were easy to get to.

MM: Well, I agree. I agree. In fact I instruct everyone who works for me to not allow me to have a firearm [laughs]. Because if I'm getting into obvious trouble, that's where it starts. If you have a lethal weapon near you, that's the beginning of stupidity — it's always the temptation. It's the Garden Of Eden; it's the fall from grace. If you see the way to destroy something, you're going to destroy it because you see how it's all been created and you get frustrated. I'm getting riled up by this conversation! You're getting transgression out of me! It's the story that will never end because there are not enough ways to shake everybody in the entire world. You can't grab everyone and shake all of them.

SP: But what about...

MM: With stuff that I said on *Antichrist Superstar* [second album]... I'm glad I said that stuff. At the time it was a great cum shot in the face of people. They were shocked and were like, 'Woah, that tasted terrible and I didn't really like that.' I'm not saying the same thing on 'Arma-Goddamn-Motherfuckin-Geddon'. I'm not even getting close to it.

SP: I'm going to change the subject here and quite cravenly appeal to your intellect by asking you to again look at transgression, not just as it applies to you but to the history of pop and rock...

MM: Okay.

SP: In the beginning, rock'n'roll was a hotbed of subversiveness, whether that was underage sex (Jerry Lee Lewis); homosexuality, or the suggestion of it when that was an absolute no-no (Little Richard); and what I guess would have been called negrophilia (Elvis Presley)...

MM: Er, did you just say negrophilia or necrophilia?

SP: Negrophilia.

11

MM: Yeah, you're correct. I'm sitting in Berlin doing this interview. I was very fascinated with Berlin because of the birth of expressionism when artists would be killed for saying, 'I'm going to paint the sky purple,' and at the same time they [the Nazis] were cursing and damning swing dancing and using expressions like that ['negrophilia'] and they were using expressions like 'the downfall of society'. They weren't around long enough to point at rock'n'roll, but they were there to point at what it came from. Last night I was stuck watching television and saw the new Eminem video in which he makes a parody of 'Jailhouse Rock' and I started thinking how relevant 'Jailhouse Rock' was to modern imagery in modern society... So I'm sitting here thinking about 'Jailhouse Rock' and thinking, 'Wow, if this video were done today it would still be unbelievably offensive.' I can't imagine what it would have been like then.

SP: Yeah, the thing about...

MM: It's all criminals, rapists, murderers, etc. dancing to this guy with a hairdo and fucking hips. It's unbelievable to me. And if you think about what is the downfall of the world — what destroyed everything — rock'n'roll did. That's where it started. Well, it is and it isn't. Rock'n'roll is the soundtrack. When they started putting it on television, that's when it became a real problem. When you combine visuals with audio, it's a very powerful medium.

SP: What about...

MM: It's propaganda. It's *Triumph Of The Will* [Leni Riefenstahl 1935 Nazi propaganda film]. It's where Wagner made opera productions that had swastikas and Hitler, who had a homosexual obsession with Wagner, said, 'I love the way that looks; I'm going to do something with that. I'm pissed off because I'm a bad watercolour artist.' Everything is about transgression. Every war. Think about nature where you have a female peacock...

SP: Peahen.

12

MM: Whatever, pick an animal. They go with a male from another tribe and then they run back to the male from theirs and he is like, 'I will defend you and I will kill everyone.' That is the central transgression, so everything is about relationships and everything is about girlfriends, and rock'n'roll defined it because rock'n'roll happened at exactly the same time as media transformed. Rock'n'roll happened when colour television was invented. Ironically, JFK was killed the week after colour television came out. Or was it ironic? I would say not. If you want to have a million-hour long conversation with me, go and look up [multinational aerospace manufacturer] Lockheed Martin on the internet. You will be so shocked. They also invented the LP record, and the colour television. They also invented satellite, and every bomb ever dropped. They invented the black box. They owned the twin towers, and the plane that flew into them. Then you become very cynical and angry about the fact that it's not a coincidence and everybody since the Roman Empire has figured out: 'Let's cause people to fight each other and let's sell them ways to do it.' And rock'n'roll became the one thing that really fucked it up for them because they weren't in charge of it. So they became in charge of it. And don't think that it's a coincidence that the people who invented all of the control invented the way to hear rock'n'roll.

SP: Who are the most important transgressive figures?

MM: Citing them? Number one: Elvis Presley. Number two: Jim Morrison. Number three: Sex Pistols. Number four: David Bowie. And that's just in my life growing up as a kid...

SP: You've just hit on something important there. When rock'n'roll started it was an assault on all fronts — underage sex, violence, death, crossing the racial divide, sexuality — but only some of these things got taken to the full extent. Why, on one hand, did Mötley Crüe get to take the heterosexual sex thing to its logical conclusion and...

MM: They didn't do a good enough job...

SP: ...and artists like yourself have explored fully the interface between totalitarianism and the rock show, but no one really has even muddied the waters of incest or underage sex or even homosexuality to any great extent? I mean, in 10 years time, will we have a rock group comprised of openly paedophilic men? They could be called The Paedos In Speedos...

MM: [laughs] It's funny you should say that because I have a [1995] record called *Smells Like Children*, you know? And I had a conversation prior to its release where I was told to take the song called 'Pretty Little Swastika' off my album. I did and this was not pandering to censorship [the track is now called 'Pretty Little $']. Their censorship choice was made purely because of money. They said, 'Take that song off your record because there are two things you can't do in music — you can never say anything anti-Semitic, and you can never say anything about paedophilia.' I said, 'Thanks for telling me that. I'm going to go ahead and combine them for you on a song and then I'm going to shave a swastika into my girlfriend's pubic hair and make her wear pigtails.' But it's not advocating either one. They're hateful! It's a statement. I didn't invent the words and symbols that everyone associates with me, and I didn't invent any sort of profanity. I wish I could make up a new curse word, but they've all been made up already. Can you blame a kid for taking building blocks with letters on them, throwing them down and having them spell out 'fuck a kid' or 'kill your parents'? No, you can't, because it's what's in your head. So raise your kids. Let them read books, and let them make their own choices. Don't tell people how to think, they get mad. And then they'll either kill themselves or kill you.

SP: Isn't the real barrier...

MM: Listen, I have to go in a second and rehearse... they're waiting for me.

SP: Look, isn't the last barrier homosexuality? People run up against it all the time — people like Bowie and yourself (and you're not even gay), and other actual homosexual rock stars...

MM: Most of them are homosexual, we just don't know it yet.

SP: Where are all the gay rock stars? Where are all the rock stars who were supposed to come out after Rob Halford of Judas Priest? If you took all the members of Metallica, Slipknot, Machine Head, Nickelback and Anthrax, I could guarantee you that at least two of those guys have had penetrative sex with another man, and fucking enjoyed it. Surely the most rebellious thing you could do if you're a musician now is to be gay?

MM: Yes.

SP: I like to think that one day we'll have another Sex Pistols moment because there's some new crunk band: four gay black rappers who perform naked with erections and then suck each off between songs.

MM: Yeah. Yeah, you're right. It is the ultimate taboo and I think it was brought up in a film that was very well done and I recommend it, called *Dahmer*, about [serial killer] Jeffrey Dahmer. They were talking about what is the most rebellious thing you can do and they said homosexuality was going against nature essentially. But it's not necessarily against nature. It only became against nature back on page 53 of the *Bible* or whatever. Sodom and Gomorrah: you've got a city named after ass-fucking, which is pretty fantastic. They burned it to the ground. I got beat up by skinheads in south Florida when I started Marilyn Manson because Nazi skinheads thought I was a Jewish homosexual; straight-edge skinheads thought I was a Jewish homosexual drug addict. It's stupid people who have just enough intelligence to read something that someone more stupid than them wrote and then they get confused and want to fight themselves, but they end up taking it out on other people. I mean I'm not gay, but I've had Twiggy's penis in my mouth. It wasn't erect and neither was mine. Neither of us are queer.

SP: Who hasn't had Twiggy's penis in their mouth?

MM: Nicely said. Who hasn't? But I'm not afraid to face that ultimate rock'n'roll thing. I like to be able to look out in the audience and see girls first and then guys. Not the reverse. But I was in the front row of a Judas Priest concert, so maybe I could have gone the other way! People, when they find out, are stupid: 'If you suck my dick I'm gonna beat your ass!' That's kind of the attitude. 'But if a gay guy sucks my dick he's a faggot!' It's aggravation and fear and that does feed a great deal of rock'n'roll music: Madonna, Prince, Bowie, everyone who has toyed with sexuality. I thought that I hadn't, but I'd forgotten all about 'Cake and Sodomy' on the first record, so I guess I've got amnesia when it comes to that. I guess I try to drink a lot so I'll forget the bad things I do. People try and get rid of the problem, but you can't get rid of it. I don't understand why people keep on trying. Every religious figure likes to do those things and it's so exposed now. Essentially that's why people become priests — because they have homosexual desires and they want to silence them. But wearing a collar doesn't stop you from being a cocksucker. And that's your pull-quote right there.

I SEDUCED THE WOMAN FOUND DEAD IN PHIL SPECTOR'S HOUSE

By MEMPHIS PIE

From issue 1, Winter 2005

I have slept with two people who are now dead. One of them was a male model that died of a heroin overdose; the other was the actress who Phil Spector stands accused of murdering.

I was visiting my mother in Hawaii early last year when I found out. I had just come in from the beach when I heard on the television that an actress had been shot at his LA mansion. "Who was it, Mom?" I asked.

"Oh, just some B-movie queen," she replied.

I walked into the room and saw a photo of Lana Clarkson, my ex-lover, on the TV screen. She was smiling a huge smile, her hair lightly blown by a fan. "Oh my God," I said.

"What?"

"Nothing."

We met on a sunny day in San Francisco when Dicky, my boss at the time, invited me out on his big red speedboat with his new girlfriend, a stupid, buck-toothed blonde stripper with the body of a 12-year-old boy. "Isn't she beautiful?" he kept asking me. "I'm thinking of buying her boobs."

Towards the end of the afternoon, we headed to Sam's, a bay-side restaurant in Marin County. All the boats were tied together so that people could roam around and mingle. On one of them was a tall, voluptuous blonde woman in sparkly jeans, high-heeled sandals and a bust-hugging sweater. She was trying to be a lot younger than she was, and that immediately attracted me to her. (When the married couple I was dating had taken me to the Swingers' Convention in Reno, the abundance of trashy, middle-aged housewives with bad perms, fake nails, thong bikinis, and stripper heels, not to mention insatiable libidos, had made me develop a fetish for women who are past their prime.) "Who is *that*, Dicky?" I asked.

"I don't know, darling," he replied. "She must be a friend of Burt's. He used to be a billionaire before the market crashed. He's got plenty of friends who look like that."

"I'm going to go seduce her. I'll be back."

"Okay, darling. Why don't you give Burt a bottle of champagne from me." (He had bought several cheap bottles earlier and put expensive price tags on. "Those assholes won't know the difference," he told me.)

I climbed over a series of 40-foot boats, at each one getting supplied with a new glass of champagne. Finally I made it to where the woman was talking to an old man with intense-looking eyes and saggy facial skin. They looked like they were fighting about something. "Hello, and welcome aboard," said the old man, trying to make his scratchy voice sound friendly. "I'm Burt, the owner of this boat, and this is Lana Clarkson, an actress visiting us from LA. Would you like some champagne?"

"Actually, Dicky wanted me to bring you this bottle."

"Tell him it's much appreciated," he chuckled. "Now let me get you a glass of the good stuff."

At that moment, a woman on the bow of the boat slipped and fell on her ass. Burt rushed over to join the other men in helping her up, and I was left alone with Lana.

I looked deeply and totally sexily into her sunglasses as we chitchatted. She replied, "Oh, is that so?" to everything I said, meanwhile checking out who she could talk to that was more important than me. "So, Memphis, would you like me to get you some more champagne?" she asked, disappearing into the cabin of the boat without waiting for an answer.

A fat man with a bright red face and a lecherous smile sauntered over to me. "I'm Captain Ned. Would you like to hear a joke?"

"Not particularly."

"Ooh! We got us a feisty one here!" he said, laughing with his mouth wide open. Then, sensing its emptiness, he shoved in some pâté and crackers. He brushed aside my hair with one of his podgy fingers and whispered, "I bet you are an animal in bed, gorgeous."

"Speaking of gorgeous," I said, "tell me about that actress."

"I don't know. She says she's in her early thirties. I think she was on *Miami Vice*. And she's got great tits!" he guffawed, his rancid whiskey and pâté breath nearly making me vomit.

I excused myself to go to the restroom and went into the cabin. Lana was sitting down talking to a man with pubic hair on his head. "I want to show you something, Lana," I said as I stood right up in front of her and began to take off my clothes to reveal my white string bikini with rhinestones on the string parts. "What do you think of my new bikini?" I asked, and I began to give her a lap dance.

She raised one eyebrow, said, "Oooh, rhinestones," and took a sip of champagne. Pubic hair was sitting there with his mouth wide open, but Lana maintained her composure. Nevertheless, I saw her lower lip tremble faintly as her perfectly manicured, slightly wrinkled hand lifted her glass to her mouth.

"I'll see you later, then," I said, picking up my clothes to leave the cabin. Neither of them said anything.

Later, as Captain Ned started the engine, Lana came up to me and said, "So how about you ditch Dicky and join us for caviar at Burt's house? He's got a pool and an excellent selection of Andrew Blake DVDs."

As we rode under the Golden Gate Bridge, I discreetly put my hand on Lana's thigh. She began to purr in my ear and said, "Are you my little kitten?"

I tried my best to purr back.

"Does little kitty like to rub pussy?"

I put my hand in her crotch.

We docked at the marina and got into Burt's bullet-proof Mercedes, which he said used to belong to a KGB officer. The market we stopped at didn't have beluga caviar, so Burt said we had to go somewhere else.

"Really, Burt," Lana whined, "it doesn't matter. Any kind of caviar is fine."

"I DON'T EAT JUST ANY KIND OF CAVIAR," he yelled with such anger that I thought he must be joking. Then I saw Lana wipe away a tear. She sulked for the rest of the ride. Ned told jokes. I was the only one who laughed.

As soon as we arrived at Burt's house in Pacific Heights, Lana led me to the bedroom and took off her clothes. She rubbed her big voluptuousness all over me, rolled around the bed messing up the high-thread-count sheets, and let her hair fall into tantalising formations in front of her face. Repeatedly, she said, "Oooh," "Aaaah," "Prrrrr," and, "My publicist would just kill me if she found out." Never once did she look me in the eye. I tried desperately to make her come but I couldn't. At one point, she got up, put on a bathrobe and said, "Caviar, little kitty?"

When we came out, Ned was smiling like a young boy on Christmas morning. Burt was glaring at the wall and didn't acknowledge us, which prompted Lana to put on her sulking face again and go sit on the other side of the room. "Why the hell do you have to be such a childish bitch?" he growled without looking at her.

Her face crumpled and she began to cry. "I'm not a bitch! Why do you say those things?"

They went into the other room, where he yelled and she whimpered for close to an hour. I had no idea what they were fighting about, but I was frightened by the intensity of it. When they came out, Lana's face was smeared and blotchy. She looked perfect.

"So, Memphis," Burt said to me seriously, "I've been thinking. You seem like a take-charge kind of woman; someone with a head on her shoulders." He shot a condescending look in Lana's direction and she started to whimper again. "I think you should work for me." His piercing eyes were looking at me as if the deal were already done.

I was scared to say yes and scared to say no. But I thought that maybe I could become Lana's protector. "One of the apartments upstairs is unoccupied," Burt continued. "You can move in next week."

Thus I began as Burt's 'personal assistant', driving his cars on errands around the city; mending his relationships with his girlfriends whenever they got in a fight; making sure the pool got swum in while he was out of town; going to New York for the Christmas party at The Plaza; buying pashminas with Wayne Newton's ex-wife, a Korean woman with the smallest nose ever constructed; taking private skiing lessons in Aspen even though I have been skiing since I was six; watching Paris Hilton make a fucking asshole of herself on the dance floor of the Caribou Club; buying Burt's daily bottle of Chopin vodka and then listening to him rant until late in the night about the shitty hand life had dealt him.

After that, when Lana came to San Francisco, she stayed in my apartment and talked excitedly about her projects and her comeback, which was inevitable, she said. She was working on a bunch of skits where she impersonated celebrities like Little Richard. Never again would she be typecast as a barbarian queen. I sat at the kitchen table with her, running my hands through her brittle, bleached hair, and gave her all my support. She always had to go to bed early and wake up early to go to work, and when she did, she would leave a sweet note with a heart or a smiley face thanking me for everything.

After a few months, Burt had grown too dependent on me and I was too scared to find out anything more about his life. When he was in Mexico with one of his girlfriends and I was supposed to be watching his house, I gathered up some of the hundred-dollar bills lying around and moved to Vietnam. I left him a note with a smiley face thanking him for everything.

I never talked to Lana again.

Phil Spector has pleaded not guilty to shooting Lana in the head. I suppose he's going to claim that she was emotionally unstable and shot herself. Yes, Lana was emotionally unstable, but I really don't think she would shoot herself. She was too full of hope and enthusiasm for her future. When she got emotional, it was to get other people's sympathy, or because she loved to create drama, like any other actress.

Of course, the good thing about all of this is that now Lana has the fame she always wanted. But I preferred her the way she was when I was first dazzled by the light of her fading star.

CAST IRON

The most cult of all rappers is called DOOM now, not MF Doom, and despite his reputation, he does sometimes let that mask slip.

By Cyrus Shahrad
From issue 21, May 2009

Any bona fide celebrity worth his or her salt tends to have at least one red button subject guaranteed to bring interviews to a less than amicable end. Jennifer Aniston, for example, refuses to talk about the fact that she's a solitary waif who sacrificed motherhood for eternally youthful hair and nails; Mariah Carey apparently storms out on anyone who dares mention *Glitter*, the trashy biopic that sped on her equally unsuccessful suicide attempt.

Hip hop writers tend to have an easier time when it comes to treading on eggshells; until last week my only exception was an interview with Kool Keith in which I was under strict instruction not to mention his much-mythologised spell in a New York mental hospital. Yet it came as no surprise to learn from his people that DOOM may be less than happy elaborating on the wilderness years that constitute the most formative and fascinating period of his career. To be honest, I was kind of expecting it.

Daniel 'DOOM' Dumile and 'Kool' Keith Thornton actually have a lot in common. Both were founding members of successful eighties and early nineties New York hip hop outfits (KMD and Ultramagnetic MCs, respectively); both dealt with the eventual commercial failure of their crews by beginning solo careers in the late nineties under surreal comic book pseudonyms (MF Doom and Dr Octagon), which over time fractured into whole strings of separate super-villainous identities (including Viktor Vaughn and King Geedorah for Dumile, and Matthew, Mr Nogatco and, wait for it, Dr Dooom for Thornton). On top of that, both are known for rapping in streams of nonsensical, abstract imagery littered with sexual and scatological humour, something that has left many interviewers keen to play psychiatrist to the voices in their heads.

As promised, Kool Keith hung up from his New York hotel room when I raised the subject of his legendary Bellevue pit stop. Yet madness per se isn't the issue most likely to rile DOOM (I'm told the capitals are also mandatory on the track names and title of his latest album, *BORN LIKE THIS.*, which also demands a full stop at the end). Instead, he's apparently loathe to discuss the period immediately following the death of his younger brother, the prodigiously talented DJ Subroc, who produced KMD's debut LP *Mr Hood*, released on Elektra in 1991, and the lion's share of their follow-up, *Black Bastards*, before being fatally hit by a car while trying to cross the Long Island Expressway in 1993.

There then followed a blow of insult to injury that most soap writers would struggle to dream up. DOOM, working under the name Zev Love X at the time, had found inspiration for dealing with his brother's death through his idol KRS-One — who refused to fold following the fatal shooting of Boogie Down Productions' DJ Scott La Rock in 1987, coming through with the seminal *By All Means Necessary* the following year — and so forged ahead with *Black Bastards* against all odds, eventually submitting a finished version of the album to Elektra in early 1994. That April, just one month before its scheduled release, a *Billboard* columnist named Terri Rossi picked up a promo copy and wrote a shockingly ill-informed piece about the cover — a deliberately jarring sketch, drawn by Dumile himself, of a stereotypical 'sambo' being lynched, a deranged grin frozen on his face. Rossi denounced as racist an image that was, even to a half-wit, completely the opposite; *Black Bastards* was a more polemic and political record than its summery predecessor, and in hanging a stereotypical sambo KMD were invoking the death of the stereotype itself.

The damage, however, had been done. Keen to avoid a repeat of the media-feeding frenzy surrounding the release of 'Cop Killer' by Ice T's Body Count in 1992 (which had led to vocal condemnation from then president George Bush Senior, among others), Elektra shelved the record and released KMD from their contract.

We're now well into the period that DOOM officially prefers not to talk about. Which is a shame, because the following years — in which a broke and basically homeless Dumile wandered the streets of New York — created a hip hop superhero (or villain, depending on your perspective) with all the literary gravity of the radioactive accidents that gave birth to the likes of Dr Manhattan or the Hulk. And when DOOM finally returned to the world of men, like the comic book legends that preceded him, he found it largely unprepared for the uncanny powers he had taken on in exile.

The story goes that these were first displayed during an open mic night at New York's Nuyorican Poets Café in 1997, when Dumile took to the stage with a stocking on his head to mask his face, stunning the crowd and savaging contenders with his abstract rhymes and intellectual, unconventional flow. Thus was born DOOM (then MF or 'Metal Face' Doom), who quickly attracted the attention of critics and label bosses alike, cornering the underground hip hop scene in what felt like a heartbeat and, in the same year, unleashing *Operation: Doomsday*, an album now widely regarded as a hip hop classic (the original 3,000 copies are collectors' items). There then followed experimental and much-admired collaborations with producers Madlib (Madvillain's *Madvillainy*, 2004) and Danger Mouse (DangerDoom's *The Mouse And The Mask*, 2005).

And all the while DOOM refused to appear without a metal mask to hide his face — something that only added to the mounting interest and internet-fuelled debate surrounding his return to the limelight. Rumours abounded that he had been facially disfigured, or that it was a cunning ploy that allowed him to sit at home watching cartoons while an army of DOOMalikes filled in at live shows, video shoots or in-store record signings. For most, however, it was simply a painfully acute metaphor; the years following Subroc's death and the split with Elektra had left DOOM emotionally rather than physically scarred. As one commentator succinctly put it: "Swearing vengeance on the industry that disfigured him, DOOM became one of hip hop's most colourful folk heroes."

DOOM's voice, when I finally get him on the phone, is surprisingly bright and breezy, light years from that of his alter ego, which seems gruffer and more aggressive with each passing release. *BORN LIKE THIS*. is no different; DOOM spits and fumes, rants and rambles, yet at the heart of the record is a fiercely poetic sensibility. By way of example, the track 'Cellz' samples an apocalyptic-sounding Charles Bukowski, whose paranoid inventory of a fearful future also gives the album its title.

"I definitely have a lot of affection for literary work," says DOOM, "especially Bukowski. I like the way he speaks through his characters; the way he roots his stories in reality but puts a fictional spin on them. I think that allows the writer and the reader to step outside the human experience, because there's only so much that a person can experience as a human. Speaking in character allows us to put a supernatural or otherworldly twist on things. I always write from an imaginary point of view, but that doesn't mean it isn't rooted in reality. It just allows me to take things to another level."

His conduit for the creative process is, not surprisingly, the mask — from the stocking that first shielded his face at his open mic homecoming in 1997, to the heavyweight metal replica of Maximus's mask from the film *Gladiator*, which has over the last eight years become as commonly associated with the 21st century's most innovative rapper as Russell Crowe's ancient Roman freedom fighter. He now has two — one in chrome, one in stainless steel — and both are heavy, forcing him to keep his head up and regulate his breathing in a way that he compares to an athlete training with arm and leg weights. But the advantages, when it comes to getting in character, are far heavier.

"I'm not one of those method actors that keeps accidentally slipping into character at the dinner table. Once I take the mask off, it's off. But at the same time, when I put it on, it's *on*, you know what I'm saying? At that point it's showtime, and sometimes even I don't know what's going to happen. It's like my whole identity shifts, like a king putting his crown on. It's a symbolic item as much as a physical one."

He says he occasionally puts the mask on at home and chases his kids around the living room — needless to say, they love it — but for most the mask is as much symbolic a barrier to the 'real' DOOM as it is a gateway for Dumile. Few of those snapping up more recent albums are old enough to remember KMD, let alone Zev Love X; for most, the only face they have to put to tracks like DangerDoom's 'El Chupa Nibre', or Madvillain's mighty 'All Caps', isn't really a face at all.

Perhaps fuelled by bitterness that DOOM refuses to let them get closer, lapsed fans air their grievances in online forums: DOOM uses the mask because he lip synchs on stage, some say; others complain that the person they saw perform wasn't really DOOM at all. Both are issues that blew up following a string of disastrous shows in the summer of 2007, which saw the performer (assuming it was actually him) the subject of boos and thrown bottles. DOOM isn't oblivious to his critics, and he's aware that coming up and shaking the hand of a man in a metal mask takes real conviction — something he says he's always quick to reward.

"I've got a lot of love for the crowd, and I'll always play to whoever is there — whether they've been following my stuff from the KMD days or know me only by my last album. And the vibe is friendly, no matter what people say: it sometimes feels like the venue is filled with more family than fans."

YouTube footage of the alleged deceptions continues to divide audiences and inspire no end of DOOM-bashing, but it's hard to imagine the man on the other end of the line capable of such tactics. Affable, articulate and perpetually self-effacing, DOOM is a million miles away from the charmless, self-obsessed rap superstar embodied by Kool Keith (who hung up on me at the first hint of a question he found compromising; DOOM, by comparison, phones me back apologetically after his mobile runs out of battery). He's also humble, casually brushing off suggestions that he's found lasting success and a core credibility that most rappers would kill for.

"As far as I'm concerned I'm still on the outside looking in. Maybe that will change with this record — maybe it'll give people something to put my name to and remember me by. Maybe not. I just try to stay positive: my focus isn't really on commercial success or acceptance. Right now, each new record feels like the first one — sometimes I think I won't be happy until I've made so many that I can't count them anymore. Either way, I certainly don't think I've reached my goal yet. I'm not sure I'll even know how to recognise it when I do."

For all that, DOOM clearly believes in his formula. The arena in which he finds himself is as fraught with peril as the one that imprisoned his masked gladiatorial predecessor, and DOOM has no intention of giving the music industry that burned him a chance to disfigure him for a second time.

"The key is to stay true to yourself: that way you know that whatever you put out will make sense and sound unique. The longer you stay on that path, the sooner people realise that you're forging something new, and the sooner they understand that something important is happening. My rule is to stick to the music side of things and let the suits and ties worry about the numbers. Because any rapper who gets too tied up in the financial side of music-making ends up being little more than a poster boy."

And hip hop, says DOOM, has more than enough poster boys. It's an understandable statement from one of modern music's most stubborn non-conformists; any artist enigmatic enough to have been remixed by the likes of Four Tet, Kode9 and Thom Yorke — the latter an ardent fan who was originally scheduled to write this article — is clearly going to rail against what he himself calls "the shit my kids listen to on MTV". More surprising, perhaps, is to hear him reflect fondly on the lowrider bicycles, block parties and bubblegum summers of 1980s New York — and in particular the soulful, blissfully innocent hip hop that first inspired him and his brother to pick up microphones.

"I remember the pair of us, aged maybe 10 or 11, staying up until 2am to record the late night radio shows and see how the beats were rocking. There wasn't even much in the way of rhyming back then — shit was mostly breakbeats with the occasional lyric on top — but we learned so much because everything was so raw and the music was developing so rapidly. Every time the show would finish we'd be sat there stunned, wondering what could possibly come next. After a while, forming KMD became the obvious way to answer that question for ourselves."

Music, he says, is memory, and his audio scrapbook of those days is more vivid than any photograph album.

"I listen to those records we made and everything comes flooding in, as though I've been transported straight back to those days. And sometimes that's not the easiest thing, because of course there were tough times along the way. But it's all part of becoming who you are, and it all makes sense when the curtain comes down. The title of the record is *BORN LIKE THIS*. No matter what you do, you were born to do it. Every atom in or out of existence is either in or out of existence for a reason, and once you accept that, you see that everything happening has already happened. I just follow the path: ups and downs, rocky roads and all. Because what else can I do?"

There's a pause on the other end of the line, as though DOOM is directing this last question more to himself than anyone else. And in that moment, it feels as though I've finally caught a glimpse of his true face.

DECONSTRUCTIVE FEEDBACK

A CD/DVD release of an orchestra improbably performing Lou Reed's
Metal Machine Music resulted in a rare opportunity to speak to
the great man, also known as 'Laughing Lou'.

By Jeremy Allen

From issue 13, October 2007

"Oh, is this interview about drugs?" snaps Lou Reed. "I thought we were here to talk about the music. Nobody wants to talk about the music anymore!"

I thought we were here to talk about the music, too, but sometimes you need to know what prompts a man to record 64 minutes of unfathomable, arbitrary, cacophonous, some would say excruciating, metallic guitar noise while doing an extremely successful impression of an international rock star. As brilliant as *Metal Machine Music* is, it would still be interesting to know what drove him to it. Was it the fact he was staying up two to three nights on the trot on a regular basis back in 1975 injecting liquid speed into his veins?

"You're not allowed to talk about drugs," interjects a female voice over the line. "You were strictly briefed on that!"

I wasn't.

"I thought we were here to talk about *Metal Machine Music*," grunts Reed.

Yes, we are. So probably not best to mention the electro shock therapy at this juncture, then.

This transatlantic phone conversation is not going at all well. The time delay only enhances the singer's frostiness. I'm already eight minutes in and I feel dirty. I feel cheapened and I feel violated. Reed's reputation precedes him, sure, but nothing can prepare you for the agonising experience of trying to engage him personally. Another journalist I know — a robust, dynamic, fearless bear of a man — also has the misfortune of talking to Reed tonight. He calls me to warn me, but it's too late. He's sat in Covent Garden nursing a coffee, hoping his hands will eventually stop shaking. Dealing with Lou Reed can leave a person traumatised.

So anyway, Lou, if you want to be pedantic, we're not here to talk about *Metal Machine Music*, the deranged feedback opus that originally got taken off the shelves after three weeks by your record company because it bombed so deliciously; the album that nearly destroyed your career and saw you living out of a hotel for a year like glam's own Alan Partridge. Technically, we're here to talk about German nutbar orchestral collective Zeitkratzer.

In 2002, Zeitkratzer did the unthinkable: they performed *Metal Machine Music* live, a feat so improbable — so audacious — that you'd think God told them to do it. And you know how improbable that is. How could anyone even conceive such a thing, let alone go through with it?

"That's what I thought," says Reed. "They got in touch to ask my permission. I couldn't see how it could be done."

But it was done. And devastatingly, too. Lou was begged by the collective to drop a cameo drone guitar over the third act of the performance and, uncharacteristically, he obliged.

"Ulrich Krieger did the transcription," continues Reed. "He said he could in fact transcribe it. They said they'd record five to 10 minutes of it and send it to me. So that's what they did. He's a very talented young man, to say the least."

When first approached, did Lou think Ulrich was, you know, a bit mental?

"No," he states. A Pinter-esque pause ensues. "I just thought it couldn't be done."

Oh.

It must have been rather thrilling to perform a work that was deemed impossible to perform and dismissed so absolutely back when it was first released.

"I was surprised at even hearing they wanted to do it."

Is Lou surprised it has become such an influential work, informing the music of Sonic Youth and just about every heavy noise band you can think of?

"A lot of things surprise me. What a wonderful surprise that was."

This is warmth.

The former Velvet Underground frontman also toured his 'difficult' *Berlin* album recently. *Berlin* was universally dismissed at the time of release but, again with the benefit of hindsight, it was reprieved and is now regarded as one of his finest works. Does he now feel gleefully vindicated?

"I felt the same about that," he offers.

Right you are. Anything else to add? No? Okay.

It occurs to me that maybe *Metal Machine Music* was a reaction to John Cale's rejection of the increasingly mainstream material that Reed had been releasing. Indeed, it could be argued that Cale was really the avant-garde one in the Velvet Underground. Reed goes nuts at this suggestion and accuses me of only being interested in celebrity and muck-raking. Bullshit. Mentioning John Cale is entirely valid. Clearly he's convinced I'm operating with some insidious agenda. I'm rattled now and I attempt to ask a question that comes out stillborn on delivery. Usually interviewees are polite enough to cut you some slack as long as it doesn't happen too often.

"I can't answer that," growls Reed, "because I don't know what the question is."

He's never one to miss an opportunity to make you feel like a turd, I'll say that for him.

Does it hurt him that his more edgy and experimental records have been shunned, while the albums he himself has admitted he's not that fond of have invariably been successful?

"I love all of my records," he lies. "I love every one of them. I don't expect people to like everything."

So here's a question he's no doubt been asked a thousand and one times, but it still has to be addressed. Lou, did you record *Metal Machine Music* to get out of your record contract?

"No. But it's such a great story, it's almost a shame to say it's not true. When people talk about me wanting to get out of a contract... I just wanted to make a guitar record with feedback solos, and not be locked into the tempo from a drum. And that was the fun of it for me. To not be trapped in a key. It's just a guitar player's album. It's so simple. Nothing complicated."

There. He got to talk about the music. It must be great inhabiting the exalted position where Lou resides — on a lofty cloud somewhere, meowing. But, as a mere mortal, I can't help feeling he abuses his status as a living legend. And the irony is, the more nasty things people write about him, the more it adds to his mystique. But really, he's just an old man with a chip on his shoulder who relishes sucking joy out of the room.

As celebrated journo John Robb, who's interviewed Reed before, told me: "The thing is he's actually quite boring. I think people expect him to be Mr Street Hassle, and all he wants to talk about is guitar effects."

You don't enter into a conversation with an artist, no matter how big or important, without believing you'll get something out of it. You arrogantly assume that maybe others have approached it with the wrong attitude, but for some reason the person will warm to you. But all I encountered was a spiteful, childish, disingenuous fucker. The exercise was ultimately a futile one. Shame. What I think I did uncover was this: maybe Lou Reed's problem is that he has no sense of humour.

CEREBRAL CAUSTIC

No boogie-woogie piano, Mr Holland. Otherwise The Fall will not appear.

By Niall O'Keeffe

From issue 10, February 2007

Who says you should never meet your heroes? Today, Mark E. Smith is charm itself. Sure, he turns up late, blaming Manchester's one-way system, but he's profuse with the apologies and grateful when I take his drinks order ("Two Coronas please!" — both for himself). He uses my first name constantly and comes off as an old-fashioned gentleman.

Yet others have gained a very different impression of Mark E. Smith. A staggering 70-odd musicians have passed through The Fall since a young Mancunian docks clerk sat down at the office typewriter in the mid-seventies and wrote his first song. The latest turn of the wheel, last year, saw three members desert a US tour. One, Ben Pritchard, publicly accused Smith of systematic bullying and heavy speed and alcohol abuse: "They're not a good mixture 'cause he'll take his speed and he'll be up for three or four days on end and all he's doing is drinking, drinking, drinking."

Today, the only indication of a dark side is the odd flash of paranoia. When I offer him another drink, his eyes narrow and he asks, "Are you having one yourself?" The implication is clear: "Are you trying to get me drunk?" Later, he fixes me with a searching look as he talks about journalists stitching him up. Generally, though, Smith seems rather like a grown-up version of the teenager who read up on the French Revolution while his father taunted him for being a "bookworm".

Driven by his autodidactic zeal, the young Smith steeped himself in music (Krautrock, sixties garage punk) and literature (Malcolm Lowry, William Blake). His refined tastes belied a fierce original-mindedness. Much is made of Smith's relentless work pace but what's more amazing is the quality of his writing: its depth, wittiness and piquancy. Look up

'Wings' or 'Hey! Luciani' and you'll discover that few people, if anyone, come close to matching Mark E. Smith as a lyricist.

When his last group mutinied, Smith recruited American replacements and, to judge from new album *Reformation Post TLC*, they've hit the ground running. So, immediately after an ugly split, a new Fall rises. With any other band, you'd consider it a Lazarus-like return. With Smith, it's just business as usual.

Smith's an advocate of primitivism and repetition. Nonetheless, The Fall's sound constantly mutates. Oddball folk punk characterised the band's first phase, which climaxed with 1982's demented classic *Hex Enduction Hour*. Dense and mysterious, Smith's writing seemed to create a whole new syntax.

After Smith's new Californian wife Laura Salenger, aka Brix, joined on guitar, The Fall embraced West Coast pop and northern soul, and a commercial golden-age ensued (see singles compilation *458489 A-Sides*). In 1989, the Smiths' marriage crumbled and Mark sojourned in Edinburgh, from where he scorned the Madchester scene: "The working class has been shafted... so what the fuck you sneering at?"

Suddenly obsessed with Italian house, Smith next recruited programmer Dave Bush and The Fall went dance, denting the Top 10 in 1993 with *The Infotainment Scan*. Two years later, as a bolt out of the blue, Brix returned, as did early-eighties drummer Karl Burns. Today, I suggest to Smith that there was a lot of potential for conflict in that mid-nineties line-up. "Tell me about it!" he replies.

Scottish artist Tommy Crooks replaced Brix on guitar, just in time to get involved in The Fall's most famous meltdown. To quote one witness of a 1998 gig at Brownies in New York: "After much antagonising from Mark, Karl jumped out from behind his kit and nearly strangled Mark. He kept saying, 'I'll kill you, you bloody cunt!' Tommy kicked Mark in the ass really hard about half a dozen times. Mark proclaimed to the audience that he had been 'assaulted by a dumb-as-a-goat Scotsman' and that we were all witnesses." The festivities continued backstage, Smith got arrested and the group went home. Court-ordered anger management deepened Smith's sense of betrayal but didn't stop him rebuilding The Fall (repeatedly).

Famously, The Fall were John Peel favourites, and the broadcaster's passing sparked a surge of mainstream interest in the group, just in time for 2005 masterpiece *Fall Heads Roll*. Arguably, this was the time to steady the ship. But, as you've probably worked out, that's not how The Fall works.

Through all this, Smith's eccentricity has generated a treasure trove of anecdotes. Former keyboardist Julia Nagle remembers him locking her in a rehearsal room overnight. When pop cultural theorist Michael Bracewell arranged a public interview with him at the ICA in 1994, a drunken Smith turned up late and demanded to be given a bucket — to piss in. Badly Drawn Boy once gave Smith a lift home, the latter having mistaken him for a taxi driver.

If you're an obsessive Fall fan, there's always another website to trawl through, another piece of gossip to savour. Still, every album or gig succeeds in chasing the trivia from your mind. Once you've tuned into this band's wavelength, most other music seems thin and pointless.

BBC broadcaster Marc 'Lard' Riley was in The Fall for a while in the early eighties. Given that Smith punched him in the face and wrote a song called 'C.R.E.E.P.' about him, Riley's assessment of the man is strikingly magnanimous: "People use the word genius quite a lot, but I do think he's a genius."

Reformation Post TLC is worthy of its place in the canon. Where *Fall Heads Roll* was dark and intense, *Reformation…* is more playful. At one point a ramshackle cover of Merle Haggard's 'White Line Fever' gives way to 'Insult Song', which good-naturedly mocks new band members. Yet there's also some real heaviness. The title track in particular throbs with malevolence; 'My Door Is Never' even threatens someone's life.

It's another great Fall record. No wonder Smith seems full of the joys as he settles down in the Malmaison hotel bar with a dictaphone under his nose…

THE STOOL PIGEON: The last group left midway through a tour and you had to find people quite quickly. Was there a period when you weren't sure the new guys were going to fit in?

MARK E. SMITH: It was a bloody fluke, really. I was so bloody lucky. Somebody up there likes me, I tell you. The English ones pissed off in fucking Arizona and two days later we had these lads. They could have been really crap, you know what I mean? Two of them were from a mate of the record company's, the drummer was freelance. He was spot on. They all lived in the same area but the drummer had never met those two. Three days after they hooked up we were playing San Diego. It is quite strange. Very strange. Because I was getting fed up with them lot.

TSP: The last lot?
MES: Yeah.

TSP: Had there been a lot of tension?
MES: Not particularly. What you find with a lot of English groups in America, they all sort of crumble after a week. They haven't got the fucking stamina. Yanks are much more... I'm going to them, 'You know there's an eight hour drive tomorrow?' and they look at you like you're mad: 'We always do that. We do that to go and see a show somewhere.' These fucking British start fucking crying. 'Is it over three hours?' They want to get on to their mams. It's true... [The Americans] are a bit more enthusiastic. Because they don't fucking know one another.

TSP: You seem to enjoy touring America. Are you fascinated with the place?
MES: It's alright to work there. I think I was determined this time. We'd cut the last tour, and every time you open a bloody newspaper there's groups quitting after a week, Oasis and that. I thought, 'This time we'll fucking do it. We're staying here, me and Elena [Smith's wife], we're staying here and we're fucking doing it.' I was really sick of it. You know what Yanks think: 'Fucking limeys, they're not rock bands.' But these [new] kids are good. They're good because — well, you've heard the record. They're fucking brilliant, actually. They're not fucking session musicians. They're 10 times better.

TSP: People assume that you are able to lick musicians into shape, instruct them.

MES: It's more the psyche of it. I restructure their ideas. They're good musicians... and I'm not a musician.

TSP: You don't really like musicians, do you?

MES: I don't, really! I don't socialise with them. Daft thing to say, but your problems arise when you start treating them like pals and they start treating you like your dad or summat.

TSP: You've shown great determination to keep playing new material rather than old stuff. Is that to ensure that there are young people at the gigs and the audience isn't ageing?

MES: The audience is getting younger and younger. I mean, at the shows we done last year there's a load of people who've never even seen The Fall before. It's good, that. We or I were sort of banned from festivals for about fucking 10 years. We've always been concentrating on being a club group. I always preferred that. But they allowed us into festivals last year.

TSP: My friend said he saw you at a Norwegian festival and you kept saying: 'We're more of a club group...'

MES: Yeah, we are. 'We're doing you a favour! Playing in the open air at five o'clock! You're fucking lucky!' Ha ha! All them other groups, they're arse-lickers, aren't they? Those festival groups.

TSP: You once said that every time you turned on your TV, you saw Primal Scream playing a festival.

MES: Ha ha! It's like a job for life, innit? Just do 20 festivals a year, earn the money, full stop. The money's good. 'New music stage: Primal Scream.' Always makes me laugh. 'New music stage: Chemical Brothers.' They've been going about 30 years, haven't they? As long as us.

TSP: You say in the opening song on the new album, 'A seven-year cycle seems to happen every day.' Is that a comment on the history of the group? Because it was about seven years after the last band left during an American tour that it happened again...

MES: It never occurred to me, that. A lot of my lyrics... half of them are on the spot, honestly. You're talking about the song 'Over' ['Over! Over!'], aren't you? The other day I had to listen to it...

TSP: Do you hate listening back to stuff?

MES: Too much, yeah. Once it's done, it's out of the fucking way and then I'm on to the next thing. I've always been like that. It's not a good thing, people say. I'm not one to fucking sit around too much, but it's funny what you said: a seven-year cycle? Did I fucking sing that? I'm more concentrated on the group and getting them over properly. I'm not saying the lyrics are secondary but... one or two songs, it's not like I'm drunk or anything, but it just came out like that on the spot. It's good sometimes.

TSP: In the early days of The Fall and through the eighties, a lot of Fall songs told very long stories and were crammed with lyrics. Have you deliberately moved away from that and tried to simplify?

MES: [snaps] Do you think so?

TSP: Well, it seems like you've sought to fragment it a bit more.

MES: Yeah, I know what you're saying — more repetition and that. I do try to hold back. It's not that I'm short of words. It is a bit conscious.

TSP: There's a song, 'Scenario', where you're singing about 'November day poppies on TV'. What's that about?

MES: A friend of mine, his dad was in the Chindits [British forces who served in Burma during World War II] and he gave me some poems of his dad's. I thought, 'This is really good shit.' And, it turns out, quite topical. Way before all this shit that's going on now.

TSP: 'The Wright Stuff' talks about *I'm A Celebrity... Get Me Out of Here!* I hear you had an approach to be on that show?

MES: Yeah.

TSP: I can't imagine that was too tempting.

MES: Ah... could have been. I was broke, I was very broke at the time. But it's a very weird thing. I remember when *Big Brother* came out, I was in this Catholic club, actually, sat with some priests, and one of them was going on, 'There's this thing called *Big Brother*...' In this Catholic club they never had the fucking TV on and I was going, 'That *Big Brother*, it won't catch on. British people won't watch that shit.' And then they went, at nine o' clock, 'Shh!' and turned the telly on! It was, like, people asleep in bed. To me, I can't understand that. The encouraging thing is, 'You were right all along, Smith: people are stupid.'

TSP: The new album seems in some ways quite playful and there's some humour on there. Is there a happy, jovial atmosphere in The Fall at the moment?

MES: Very much. It's a big difference. Very self-important, Manchester musicians, as you can imagine. London musicians are pretty easy-going, but in Manchester, they think they're really great. I've never seen The Fall as a Manchester group. We've always been at arm's length.

TSP: I guess the closest thing you'd have to a peer here is John Cooper Clarke. Is he a mate?

MES: He was a mate, and he did play at some of our shows. He's a mate of the Arctic Monkeys now! I actually read that thing in *Mojo* [an interview with Clarke conducted by Monkeys singer Alex Turner]. I didn't read about me — this is the sort of person I am — I read that one just to get the humiliation... I'm going to wind him up if I ever see him again. He's a fucking space cadet, that Monkey guy! It's funny, Clarke licking up to him. He's got the support slot on the tour now! What's that about?

TSP: Regarding the internet, do you find the level of interest in The Fall and the amount that The Fall gets discussed on the internet almost a bit troubling?

MES: It's half-truths, innit? There's about three fucking websites for The Fall. If I spent me time reading it I wouldn't have time to do anything else. But Elena checks in on it and the group are pretty well up on it.

TSP: But you feel you have better things to be doing?

MES: I don't like reading about myself. I never have. Total strangers know more than I do. What amazes me is, a lot of journalists I talk to, the big papers, they take it as gospel, which I find really weird. Some bloke from Hartlepool can say I was in a boozer in Hartlepool with some woman, and someone from the fucking *Times* will be like, 'Oh, you were in Hartlepool the other night.' I'm like, 'No I fucking wasn't.' Some nut case, pissed out of his head, has put, 'I saw Mark Smith the other night...' like people do. And they take it as bloody gospel. It's quite strange.

TSP: Have you any views on MySpace culture?

MES: What, MySpace? There's another one that's got, like, three tracks...

TSP: On MySpace you can put four tracks up...

MES: What, of The Fall?

TSP: A lot of bands have set up MySpace sites, and you can link to other people's sites...

MES: Are we on that?

TSP: I don't think there's an official Fall one...

MES: There's an official one and an unofficial one.

TSP: Those are websites. There's also this MySpace thing, which is a networking site...

MES: I think we're on that. Sanctuary did ask me. I think it's on. Because somebody told me the other day, another stranger, that it was the one where they hung Saddam...

TSP: YouTube?

MES: They hanged Saddam and then The Fall's 'Insult Song' comes on right after it. Ha ha! That's not very nice, is it?

TSP: What did you think of the hanging of Saddam Hussein?

MES: Me? I was very deeply ashamed. And I don't usually get worked up about politics. I was very deeply ashamed. And you just know what Blair's going to say: 'Well, Iraq has the death penalty,' when, every time they hang any fucking body around the world, or kill anybody, there's always a petition at the embassy, isn't there? Saying, 'We don't agree with the death penalty,' and all this. I was upset, actually. The wife was very upset. She's like, 'I wanna leave.' And I can understand that.

TSP: You mentioned Tony Blair. What's your view on the succession, Gordon Brown taking over from Tony Blair?

MES: I think people get the fucking government they deserve, really. You get me? I mean, there doesn't seem to be any opposition in this country. I think the sinister thing is, the opposition is very glad to be in the opposition. They're all pals, aren't they? I'm not saying they should hate each other, like Hitler and the Communists or something, but no fucker's bothered. You open a newspaper, it's like, Jordan's on page one; Chelsea players on page three; page six, 10,000 Iraqi women and kids have been bombed by accident. I find that really worrying, that. I'm not going to go on about the Iraqi war, but I didn't like that hanging, me. There are British soldiers out there, you know? And apparently in Britain we don't believe in death by hanging. It went out when I was a fucking kid. The last hanging was in Strangeways, which is a fucking five-minute walk from where I fucking live; from where I was born. I find that very worrying.

41

TSP: When you go to the States, do you find that it's become a more right-wing place with Bush in charge?

MES: What really shocked me is, when we were in Texas, they hate him. They hate Bush! I don't mean people at gigs, I mean rednecks! It's like, 'Fuck Bush,' and all that. Not particularly because of the Iraq war. It's just, they don't fucking like him. You think, 'If only we had a bit of that here.'

TSP: Do you think people are too accepting of Tony Blair?

MES: They get what they fucking deserve, in my book. There's no use tossing and turning about it... I personally wanted to fucking line them up against the wall in 1998 and fucking shoot the lot. But I've got a bit of pre-cog like that. People, semi-friends, wouldn't talk to me: 'You've really lost it now, Mark.'

TSP: You've claimed to have pre-cognitive powers for years, with a number of things: you wrote 'Powder Keg' before the Manchester bombing, 'Terry Waite Sez' before his kidnapping... Do you get freaked out when events transpire to give a song new resonance?

MES: I try not to think about it, really. Because my mam was a bit psychic. I was, very much, when I was a teenager. But it's not a good gift to have. First up, people think you're fucking barmy. Second thing is, a psychic can forecast when a bus isn't going to arrive but they can't forecast the winner of a horse race. It's no good to you! It's not much fucking use if you can't forecast how to win the pools. So I've always thought that, since I was 20. It's something that's there, you know. It gets a bit horrible sometimes.

TSP: You're afraid to say what you think might happen?

MES: I can see, with a journalist... I know if he's going to stitch me up. And there's no reason for it. You know what I mean? It's not a very nice thing to know.

TSP: A couple of years ago, with the BBC4 documentary and with

John Peel's passing, there was suddenly a lot of interest in The Fall...

MES: I did spend two fucking years building the group back up again, which is why them fucking off on me pissed me off. I mean, seriously. Two years of fucking hard slog to get *Fall Heads Roll*, that LP. It was fucking hard work, that, tutoring people and getting them into the psyche of it... The reputation of me in the group was, like, in the year 2000 I could hardly get shows. 'He's a fucking drunken nutcase, gonna kill you if you put him on.' It's all right laughing now, but... The thing about me and Peel is I only spoke to him about four times ever. I always told him we never depended on him, and he knew that, God bless him. If we'd depended on John Peel, we would have starved to death. We never counted on it. He knew that. I don't think we're ever going to get on the BBC again, actually.

TSP: You did *Later... with Jools Holland*. There was a story going around that you insisted Jools stay away from his piano when you were playing. Any truth in that?

MES: I did put a clause in there. It's true what they said. I tried not to admit it, but it was fucking true. It was, like, Clause 11: 'No boogie-woogie piano, Mr Holland. Otherwise The Fall will not appear.' It was very funny. And I walked in to do the soundcheck and I sort of vaguely know his drummer, and he just got up and walked out! Jools Holland walks past and I go, *'Hey Jools, y'alright?'* and he fucking runs off! They take it dead serious, don't they?

TSP: Does it annoy you when a lot of focus is put on ex-members of the group? In *The Guardian*, for example, Dave Simpson did a big piece on everybody who's ever been in The Fall.

MES: No, it wasn't their fault, actually... I had the guy [Simpson] in here, actually. I thought he wanted to talk about the LP. He kept going, 'What's happened to blah blah?' I'm going, 'I don't fucking know.' After two hours, he fucking cracked! [mimes crying] 'I've had enough of this! I can't get anything out of you!' I'm saying, 'Have you heard the LP or not?'

TSP: He was emotional? Teary?

MES: Yeah, yeah. I did pile him up a bit.

TSP: With drinks?

MES: Yeah. Me old tricks. Couple of whiskies and that. Always works. Then I took him to a pub over there [across the street] and I got it all out of him. What it was, his boss had said to him: 'Get the dirty on Mark E. Smith.' The editor. Because he [Simpson] used to have an office in London. Then they had a bit of cutback. He was kept on, but he had to go back to Yorkshire. He was still working for them. They said, 'You've got to get a fucking scoop.' Get the dirty on me! It must have cost a fortune, that piece. The ex-members, I don't know where they live...

TSP: The only guys he didn't find were Johnnie Brown and, more significantly, Karl Burns.

MES: I'll tell you a funny story about that. As he was going back to the train station, we went in this other pub by which time I'd got more out of him than he'd got out of me. But, as we went in this fucking pub, I couldn't believe it, there was this woman sat there in the fucking pub with her boyfriend. It was fucking Karl Burns's mum! She said, 'Mark! How've you been?' I says, 'Hello Mrs Burns, nice to see you.' She's like, 'Long time no see.' And he gets his fucking pad out! 'What is Karl Burns doing now?' She goes: 'I don't know, he does what he bloody does.' 'What's his address?' 'Oh, he lives on a farm in the hills somewhere, looks like that bloke out of *Emmerdale*...' Ha ha!

TSP: Alongside that documentary and that article, there were various books written as well.

MES: Yeah. All crap.

TSP: Did you read Simon Ford's one, *Hip Priest*?

MES: No. I can't, really. It's not that I can't be arsed, it just might affect you. I've always been like that. I don't read much about myself.

Maybe I should, I don't know. That Mick Middles one, I didn't get past page 50. A lot of those books, I think it's more about the person who's writing it. Do you ever get that impression? It's like the people who write them history programmes — they write about Cromwell and they look like Cromwell, don't they? They get a bit too involved in their subjects.

TSP: There's a good Raymond Chandler quote in *The Independent* today: 'The more you reason, the less you create.'
MES: Yeah, that's spot on, actually.

TSP: Chandler was an influence on the young Mark E. Smith, wasn't he?
MES: What, on the young one? Yeah. I'm more into Jim Thompson nowadays. You know, he did *The Getaway* and everything pulp fiction and that shit tries to be... But I agree with what Chandler says. It's kind of like reading about yourself, listening to music... I don't try to listen to music a lot, otherwise The Fall has no purpose. I do watch groups on the TV now, only because they've got one of them things for deaf people and you get the lyrics of the songs, and it's fucking hilarious. It cheers me up. I don't feel so bad then. How appalling the lyrics are... It's like, 'It's not that bad, Mark. Your writing isn't that bad, cock.'

TSP: Your own memoir, *Renegade*, is on the publication schedules now. Did you just feel that you wanted to put those other books out of business?
MES: Yeah, that was the original idea for it. It's nowhere near finished. I've got a ghostwriter. The thing is, I'm not a book-writer... I do bits and bobs, but I think it takes a lot of discipline and concentration, and of course everything's on the records, so sometimes things have to take preference. But it's shaping up alright. I want to make it a bit different. I don't want to just shove it out. I'm thinking of doing it like a football biography. It would be a parody on that, which would be funny. 'Chapter 6. I remember my first gig. I was gobsmacked. We only got £15.50 that night...'

TSP: Do you have axes to grind with certain past members of the group?

MES: I've tried not to bring it up, really. Actually, I lie: I'm trying to work on these interludes where the groups fuck off on me or I fuck off on them. You know: 'New York, 1998...' That sort of shit. Like them daft novels, you know, Jackie Collins, Thomas Harris. 'Flashback!'

TSP: With that 1998 thing and this latest walkout, did you feel a sense of betrayal?

MES: I should call the book 'Betrayal'! 'The Betrayal of St Mark'!

TSP: There's been this suggestion that you like to keep the band on their toes and maybe bully them a bit... I read a quote where you said that you sometimes give them the wrong directions to the studio so that they arrive pissed off and play better. Is that a philosophy you bring to bear a lot?

MES: Depends who it is.

TSP: Do you think certain players respond to that?

MES: Well, a lot of players don't react very well to it, obviously.

TSP: Have you had any contact from that last lot?

Elena Poulou [who's just joined us]: They called up before Christmas: 'I'm sorry.'

TSP: Ben Pritchard seemed quite a solid member of The Fall. It was quite surprising to a lot of people when he left...

MES: It's always the ones you least expect, in my experience...

TSP: He did a couple of interviews after he left the band.

MES: Yeah, I saw them. I got them taken off the net. They were libellous. What a load of ridiculous rubbish. I had to ring his dad up and say, 'Get it off!' To me, it was nothing, but he was talking about other people, who were very upset, like me sister and Elena. No need for it.

It's not fair... There's a lot of myths [about the band's various splits]. It's like, half the time they left me. It looks better to say you got fired. Half the time, they weren't up for it. There's shit I could have said about them, you wouldn't fucking credit it. I would never do it. I'm a gentleman.

TSP: From the Simpson piece, it seemed that a lot of ex-members kind of missed being in The Fall.
MES: The two-year gap, I call it.

TSP: They get out and two years later they think, 'What have I done?'
MES: Yeah.

TSP: Do you think you're getting that with Pritchard and that lot at the moment?
MES: Yeah. I wanted to call the book 'Two-Year Gap'. But Penguin wouldn't have it.

THE MYSTERY OF THE GALLOWBIRDS

Vile swamps! Exploding birds! And the suspected involvement of Friedberger siblings, known to most as The Fiery Furnaces. A true tale of horror and intrigue stretching two continents.

By Phil Hebblethwaite
From issue 1, Winter 2005

The plan was to talk about their music and then move on to what happened. Ten minutes in and Nathan wasn't happy with how things were going. I could tell by the way he was looking at me and slapping the back of his neck with his fingers. He nodded, stood up and drew the curtains in the chalet. That was my cue. "Don't be afraid," I said, "and don't think we're mad, but there's something else we want to ask you about — something weird we need you to consider and respond to."

The brother gave a hesitant, drawn-out "okaaaaaay". His sister smirked and leaned forward in her grey, plastic chair. "What is it?" she asked.

"I'm going," I said, "to tell you about the birds."

Six months earlier, Nathan and I were in New Orleans. We'd met an all-round good guy called Alex who'd let us crash on his floor in the uptown part of the city. He was a skater and a party maker who made good money throwing a weekly eighties night down on Tchoupitoulas Street.

It was on the morning of our last day in New Orleans when we asked Alex if he would take us to see the wooden house he'd built for his mother out on the swamps. We left after breakfast and picked the soundtrack for the journey by a process of elimination. Only I had brought records and we'd blasted to death all but one. "Looks like it has to be The Fiery Furnaces," I said, and neither Nathan nor Alex objected.

We were already outside the city by the time I mentioned that band. A downpour the night before had left the swamps bulging and spilling a thick, brown sludge onto sections of the smaller roads. They, like the locals who stared at us with suspicion as we drove past, looked unwelcoming. The landscape was harsh out there and it was scarred by the rusting cars and trash that had been left to sink into it.

I'd never listened to the Fiery Furnaces record before that trip. It's hard to explain why. I'd come across them when they played at their label's 25th birthday party in London and I liked many things about them — their circus-like sounds, how imaginative and odd the lyrics were and, most memorably, their lead singer. She ensnared everyone that watched. Away from the mic she seemed so sweet and vulnerable, but when she sang she became menacing and powerful and deeply unsettling.

This is what I discovered about the band after the gig: that they were a brother and sister outfit originally from near Chicago who used a hired drummer and bassist. Brother Matthew seemed to write the music and his little sister, Eleanor, the words. That was it. There was a biography on their label's website, but it'd clearly been written by them and was designed to tell people as little as possible about who they really are.

Instead, I started keeping an eye out for other gigs they were playing in London. There was one in Islington and another at The Metro on Oxford Street. I attended both, only to return home in a disturbed state of mind. It was a love affair of sorts I was having with them, but I didn't understand their music and they were beginning to freak me out. Matthew's compositions, which he seemed to rearrange constantly, were impressive but odd and Eleanor was becoming more and more distressing. When she sang, she stared gun-barrel-eyed out into the audience as if they weren't there. People would think she was looking at them, but it seemed to me like she was temporarily, horribly lost — in some kind of trance or nightmare.

You could tell by observing this brother and sister that they were good-natured and kind people and the interviews with them that began to turn up in the press suggested the same. I never thought they were evil, just that their music had some sort of extra quality that was out of control and impossible to reason with. I don't believe in the supernatural, but there was nothing else I could fall back on. And the name of their album, *Gallowsbird's Bark*, confused me, too. A gallowsbird is someone who deserves to be hanged. But who were they referring to?

When I told Nathan and Alex about the band, they said they were excited to hear their record. I remember Nathan saying, "Let's fucking play it," so that's what we did — we fucking played their record — and just as we did, from nowhere, an enormous bird — an eagle — dropped from the sky, landed on the cables of an electricity pylon and burst into flames. It was daytime, but the flash of blue light was blinding. When it dimmed, the blackened carcass of that poor bird rocked for a second and then plunged deep into the swamps.

"What the..." said Alex. Nathan cackled. I felt terrorised. My mind searched for sense. Was this destined to happen? Was it a coincidence? A warning? When we arrived at Alex's mother's house, Alex and Nathan pissed about and drank beer. I sat on the small wooden jetty in the backyard smoking cigarettes and watching tiny fish dart around in the swamps.

Time is a soother, of course, and it helps you reason with the bizarre. Over the next few months, I gazed for hours at the wolf's head and noose on their record's cover and listened to it obsessively. Nothing else strange occurred. The incident with the eagle, I persuaded myself, was an accident of nature and unconnected to *Gallowsbird's Bark*. I began to deride myself for ever thinking otherwise.

And I kept attending their gigs. At one in Highbury & Islington, I met a man from their record label. He asked whether I was going to All Tomorrow's Parties on Camber Sands in Sussex a fortnight later. I was, so he gave me his number and asked me to call when I got there. The idea was to come round to the band's chalet after their performance for a drink and a chat.

Road trips are fun, even if you're only going a short distance. On that journey from London to Sussex, Nathan and I stopped and ate shit food at some service station and sang like a pair of idiots all the way through Kent. We were listening to Eddie Cochran, and when Eddie was through, Nathan suggested we play the Fiery Furnaces record. It was to be the first time he'd heard it since the trip to New Orleans.

What happened next caused the blood to drain from our faces. We were a moment through the first song on the album and travelling at 70mph when another vast bird — a crow this time — swooped in front of the car clutching a lump of earth in its beak. Inexplicably, it hovered above of us for a second, then released its load and glided off. All I can remember of the next moment is trying to swerve out the way. I couldn't. The lump of earth thudded into the exact middlepoint of our windscreen and dispersed into a million fragments.

• This time, Nathan didn't laugh. He trembled and released a slow and painful groan. I felt sick. As soon as I could, I pulled over and, with a hand on my twisted guts, spoke: "The band must be held to account for what has just happened! I can excuse one terrible incident, but another is too much!" Nathan agreed. That crow, we decided, had delivered an omen that only The Fiery Furnaces could explain.

We watched their performance at All Tomorrow's Parties from the back of the hall. I noticed that they'd recruited another new drummer who was better than the last one and they played tight, but little else. It was hard to concentrate. We drank heavily throughout the show and watched the audience more than the band. When they finished, we waited for exactly an hour and then we walked over to Chalet 54 and knocked on the door.

I began by asking why their record was called *Gallowsbird's Bark* and Matthew said he thought their songs were "scoundrel" songs and the songs themselves deserved to be hanged and, in fact, they enjoyed creating "defence mechanisms" around themselves and that was why they'd written such disparaging things about each other when their record label had asked for their biographies. We spoke about their show, too, and they said they liked to rearrange their songs every month or so to prevent routine setting in.

Then I told them about the birds.

Matthew was first to speak. "The bird today was a crow?" he asked and I said that I assumed so; that I could be 90 per cent sure it was a crow. Then he said, "If it was an eagle..." and I tried to stop him but he was thinking out loud and saying things like, "If it was an eagle dropping a cub, it would be..." and he mentioned how the eagle is a Roman symbol and the cub was Rome itself because Rome is being suckled. And he said the word "twins", too, and I thought perhaps he was thinking of Romulus and Remus but nothing he was saying was making much sense so I stopped him. "Matthew, the bird in New Orleans was an eagle. Today, we saw a crow and it didn't drop a cub — it dropped a piece of earth."

"Okay, fine," he said and sank his head into his hands. Silence. Nathan still seemed anxious. I felt disappointed and embarrassed. I wanted to go. "Listen, not to worry," I said and suggested leaving. But Matthew wouldn't let us.

"No!" he suddenly shouted. "The crow is a symbol for rural Britain!"

I froze. Rural Britain? "Why?"

"Because it's a nice, calming bird."

"But this bird was hideous."

"They're smart, though," he said. "Crows are very smart. And they *are* calming."

He seemed sure and it was comforting. Perhaps the bird hadn't been so awful after all. Maybe my mind really was playing tricks on me. Rural Britain. Rural Britain. Rural Britain. What? I didn't understand him and I didn't feel content. Neither was Nathan. "So what if that bird is a symbol of rural Britain," he said. "We need to know why it dropped that lump of earth on our car."

"Okay, fine," Matthew said, and a blankness fell over his face.

"Come on, let's go," I said, but again Matthew stopped us. His expression changed, then he clicked his finger and rose from his chair. "The soil of England was dropped on your car today!" he bellowed. "The legacy of your country has been dumped in your lap!"

He was triumphant and it stirred Eleanor. "What are you going to do with it!?" she shrieked. "What are you going to do with it!?"

"It's up to your generation..." Matthew said.

"Carry on!" I roared.

"...to take up the challenge and make Britain a cultural beacon to the world once more!"

The four of us sat back in our chairs. I looked at Nathan. He exhaled, clapped his hands together and nodded. I think he may have smiled, so we thanked The Fiery Furnaces and we left their chalet, and we drank lots more ale that night, and we lost our minds, and we danced and we danced and we danced until there was no more music, and then we slept the sleep of a thousand men.

ALOHA FROM HELL

The grave tale of a dead serious rock'n'roll band, The Cramps.

By Garry Mulholland

From issue 9, December 2006

"We've been written off as kitsch, camp, cartoony. But we're dead serious." Poison Ivy Rorschach is not a woman to argue with on this kind of point. Not that the 52-year-old guitarist and co-founder of the living legend that is The Cramps is in any way testy, aggressive or bitchy, despite all those sneering leopard-skin dominatrix poses she's struck over the last 30 years. But she knows what she knows, loves what she loves, and has earned the right to let her point stand many times over.

Ivy is the historian of the incredibly strange band she formed in 1975 with the love of her life, Lux Interior, the Herman Munster of vintage minimalist rock'n'roll. If you've never heard The Cramps, or have but don't understand what an impact they've had on global pop culture, then let me introduce you to the human interest element of the Lux'n'Ivy saga. They are one of the great love stories of rock. Met on a California freeway in 1972, fell for each other instantly, have not spent a day apart in 34 years. The couple that plays together, stays together, particularly if what they play is mondo-gonzo dirty blues punk rock'n'roll shot through with the vivid colour, satire and sex of fifties teen culture, stoopid-dumb B-movies, vintage pornography, Vegas Elvis, backwoods rockabilly, sicko sixties garage, iconic burlesque clothing, pink Cadillacs, dirty doings at the eternal American drive-in, Ms Spanks-a-lot Amazonianism, Ed Wood sci-fi and the kind of gratuitous filth that only the most romantic people on the planet can indulge in and understand that the filth is the love, L.U.V. They are The Cramps. And they transcend rock'n'roll because they are a genre of their own.

We're talking to Lux and Ivy because... well, actually, because they're the goddamn Cramps, f'chrissake! They have no product to promote, no new album. They have just finished remixing and remastering their 1979 *Gravest Hits* mini album, to be reissued next year with a slew of previously unreleased tracks from their first legendary Memphis recording sessions. And they have just finished a tour, mainly festivals. "I really enjoy that," says Lux, "because you look out at all the faces and you can tell they've never seen you and don't know what to expect." Lux says everything with a kind of goofy drollness, reminiscent of James Stewart and the way The Greatest Film Actor Of All Time could use his down-home drawl and easy likeability to deliver stinging sarcasm while remaining eminently loveable.

Talking to Lux and Ivy about their extraordinary past is not just obvious, but appropriate, because the past is where they live. Or, as Lux sees it: "At the time when we started, and even today, you hear people say, 'We want to do something new. We don't wanna have anything to do with the past.' Well, that's okay, but you sure get a lotta crap that way."

So let's get right into that backstory. It is 1972, and an average day on an average highway outside Sacramento, California. A 26-year-old Ohio student called Erick Lee Purkhiser is driving with a friend. They spot a female hitchhiker and gallantly pull over. An 18-year-old Sacramento student called Kristy Marlana Wallace gratefully accepts a lift.

Ivy: "Everyone hitchhiked in California at that time. It was a very hippy era. We all thought it was safe, but it was hare-brained, looking back. I think we would have met anyway. It was destiny."

So Lux, you pick up this hitchhiker and she turns out to be the woman you'll not just be with, but work with, and create an entire aesthetic world with for the next 30 years of your life. One would imagine that there must have been some kind of psychic earthquake when you first looked at each other. Was there?

"Yes. It was exactly like that. She was somebody really special when I met her, we immediately got along and we've never spent any time apart since. She's just... smart, and interested in all the things that I was

55

interested in. When we first met, all we wanted to do was go to rock'n'roll shows. And at that time, going to rock'n'roll shows in southern California was great 'cos everybody got dressed up like crazy and... it almost didn't matter who the band was. The audience was more interesting than the bands. I'd wanted to be in a band and she played guitar and we got this idea within days of meeting each other: that we should have a band."

But let's not get ahead of ourselves. It took a while for this idea to reach any kind of reality, and it didn't happen in Sacramento, where, in one of a set of bizarre post-hitchhike coincidences, Erick and Kristy happened to be enrolled in the same art class. It was Art and Shamanism. Of course it was. Ivy: "The primary text book for it was a book called *The Sacred Mushroom And The Cross*. It said that the *Bible* was a hidden code for magic mushrooms. I didn't see Lux until the next semester. He walked in the class and I said, 'Sit by me, sit by me!' It was my birthday and he gave me a drawing as a present. And then the next time we met in class we ended up sticking together for ever and ever."

What happened next is that Lux and Ivy up and moved to Lux's hometown of Akron, Ohio in 1973. "There was a, uh, legal issue in California," Ivy recalls, darkly. "But I don't want to elaborate on that. We just had to get out of town."

Their mysterious flit turned out to be fortuitous. Akron is one of those apparently anonymous small towns which over-achieved in the field of punk/new wave/art rock and all that. Chrissie Hynde and Devo are both Akron alumni, and Pere Ubu were stationed just down the road in Cleveland. Ivy: "Akron was very inexpensive to live in. So we had this gigantic three-storey house for the two of us. We used the attic for rehearsals. We must have talked about the band in Sacramento, though, because I actually bought Lux the fuzz pedal we use, which is a Univox Superfuzz, from a pawn shop. His brother sent him a Student Prince guitar and I taught him 'Baby Strange' by T.Rex.

"We were both working in a circuit-board factory. Really boring. A really fascist boss. We weren't cut out for that kind of work; we're too delicate and sensitive. Although, one of the early interviews we did was with Nick Kent, a really cool writer, and he thought we said surfing-board factory. I kinda hate to say that's not true, 'cos I imagine we'd be sanding and waxing surfboards. That's too cool.

"Through record collecting we were getting more and more passionate. Being exposed to music that most people weren't. There wasn't much going on in the seventies that really thrilled us... the New York Dolls had broken up, T.Rex wasn't what it was before. I think being together — not just as a couple, but as partners in crime — that you can get each other wound up in a way that a person alone can't. We convinced each other that it was a viable option to have our own band and that everybody would think it was really cool. It was kind of a delusion. Except that we succeeded with it."

What Lux and Ivy were doing, at this point, was developing a perfect pop-art aesthetic, an amalgam of pop-cultural trash elements drawn from fifties rock, B-movies, glam, and the original sixties strain of punk rock. Ivy: "It was a natural, organic thing. People think we're more image-conscious than we are... it's really more self-expression of our personal tastes. And we didn't know who else would be in the band — we didn't know anyone who even knew who The Sonics were, and they were a must as an influence. We had to do rockabilly songs. When we first went into the basement of the Musical Maze record store with Bryan Gregory and his sister Pam to jam, we didn't know how we'd sound. So we just did it. We didn't have enough going on to discuss it! When we met Bryan we just connected. It was a chemistry thing. There was never a plan."

But if it was so organic, how did little Erick and Kristy wind up with those brilliantly conceived stage names?

"I was Poison Ivy in Sacramento. I still have a driver's licence that says that, and this was before any thought of a band. Lux was Flip Flop on his driver's licence. When we went to Ohio, he was Raven Beauty and eventually changed to Lux Interior. For some reason that doesn't make sense to me now. I thought I needed a last name, and Rorschach [named after the inventor of those infamous 'inkblot' psychiatric tests] came to me in a dream. But I was already Poison Ivy before The

Cramps. We were reinventing ourselves, but not because of the band. Only our shrink knows why."

The first completed Cramps line-up from 1975 featured Lux, Ivy, guitarist Bryan Gregory (The Cramps, famously, were the first primal rock'n'roll band to dispense with bass) and Bryan's sister Pam Ballam on drums. But even though Akron produced great bands, the fledgling Cramps were not part of the cool art rock scene. "One thing people assume," Ivy continues, "is that we knew those people. We didn't. We weren't aware of them playing, except that we saw Rocket From The Tombs [precursors to Pere Ubu] supporting Television in a hotel in Cleveland. We didn't meet any of them until we moved to New York. We didn't know anything in Ohio except our stupid jobs and mainstream gigs. We didn't know there was an underground. So we had to get out of there."

In America at that time, there was really only one place for a pack of proto-punk weirdoes to move to. In September 1975, The Cramps hit New York. Ivy again accesses her total recall and sets the scene. "We'd done the nine-hour drive from Akron twice and seen the Ramones and Television, so we knew it was all there. Get a few days off, take speed, drive there, see the bands, drive back and there'd be nothing left of us when we got back to Ohio. But those two trips convinced us we had to move. We had enough money for a hotel for two days, and couldn't find a place to live. So we slept the third night in the car at a truck-stop in New Jersey and said, 'If we don't find somewhere tomorrow, we'll have to forget it and go back to Ohio.' That day we found our apartment. So we moved and proceeded to starve. But that was okay. We had to be there."

The 1975 lightning conductor that was Hilly Kristal's CBGBs, which finally closed its doors in October 2006 — yet another victim of the post-Giuliani disinfecting of New York culture and nightlife — provided instant focus and opportunity for the nascent Cramps, as they quickly found like-minds, got gigs and printed up the posters and flyers that invented the term 'psychobilly'.

"It was easier than you'd imagine," reckons Ivy. "That's why we feel so grateful and so fortunate with the scene that was there at the time. Monday night was audition night at CBGBs, but not everybody could get on. We did straight away because we'd made friends with The Dead Boys, who were really hot at the time. So The Dead Boys headlined this audition night, and we played our first show to a packed house. A lot of people saw us, as chaotic as we were, including Peter Crowley who booked Max's Kansas City. He loved us and immediately booked us. Hilly Kristal thought we sucked, which we probably did. But Peter loved us and we started playing Max's regularly, supporting Suicide. We got a following just from that. We put these flyers up all over town and that's where the 'psychobilly' tag came from... we thought it up just to get people interested in us. We clicked straight away. The biggest break was when the Ramones saw us, and dug us, and then they let us open for 'em. Their audience loved us. New York was just a magnetic Mecca for people and there was just this swell of energy. We were hanging out at CBGBs and Max's every night of the week, and so was everybody else. A swirl of creativity. It must be so hard for bands now. People are much more jaded."

Supporting two of the counter-culture's most influential bands also helped The Cramps find their own peculiar X-factor. "The Ramones were just like this blast of light onstage. The energy influenced us. And Suicide's Alan Vega intimidating the audience. He showed us that antagonism could be fun."

I ask Ivy if the story of her working as a New York dominatrix was truth or fiction. "That's true. It was a very interesting time. I was making way more money than anyone else in the band. And the work suited me. We didn't struggle in the way we would have if I'd just stayed waiting tables. It enabled us to be independent."

I realise more salacious info is not immediately forthcoming. I prod, warily... So, no horrible, sleazy nightmare moments from your stint in the sex industry?

"No, not at all. I was cut out for the work."

There is a finality about the statement. Guess we'll have to wait for the uncensored autobiography.

Nevertheless, the initial filth and fury of punk rock had pretty much come and gone before The Cramps, now with Pam Ballam replaced by Nick Knox, made their first record. For the 1978 sessions that became *Gravest Hits*, the rockabilly obsessives went straight to the source — Memphis — with Box Tops/Big Star cult legend Alex Chilton as producer. With half of the sessions recorded at Phillips Recording, the post-Sun studio owned by Sam Phillips, the man who didn't just discover Elvis Presley, Johnny Cash and Jerry Lee Lewis, but signalled the birth of the modern world by putting out records by fifties legends both black and white on the same label, from the same studio. Were the novice Cramps in awe? Lux: "By that time we had almost collected every Sun label single. We'd gone to the Sun warehouse. When I first met Ivy we drove all the way across the country to visit Memphis. So we were really in awe of that building and Sam Phillips. And then we met him. We had to stay overnight in the studio because we got locked in and we met him. It was like a dream or something. Could this be happening? We were told he never comes to the studio, but he showed up with a chainsaw to cut down the vines that had grown up over his name plaque. It was a magical experience."

What was he like? "A million laughs. We didn't talk to him too much. But we told him that we had every Sun single, and he says, 'Well, you know something?' And we said, 'What?' And he just says, 'You're lucky.' He had these huge glasses on that magnified his eyes until he looked like a monster from outer space. He's a real character."

The first flurry of Cramps releases, from 1978's debut single, 'The Way I Walk / Surfin' Bird', through to 1981's *Psychedelic Jungle* album, remain the band's greatest, and felt like a punch in the gut at the time. The Cramps found a way to merge the wildest backwoods rockabilly of the fifties and the freakiest beats of the sixties with the art punk of the late seventies, allying a comic sexual mania with white noise feedback fuzz and a feral rhythmic buzz that seemed to sum up every rebel rock genre that had ever made a square squeal, "But that's not music! It's just noise!!!" at a budding teenage hedonist who really didn't care because they'd just been shown a place better and realer than the so-called real world. But even as legions of kids — particularly in Britain and Europe — fuelled a rockabilly revival, adopted and adapted the term psychobilly, merged The Cramps' horror show threads with their own punk or goth or futurist accessories, and made 'Human Fly' and 'Garbageman' into hardy alternative clubbing perennials, the band were facing two major crises which would prevent them taking advantage of their instant cult status and scoring mainstream hits.

The Cramps had signed to I.R.S., the label owned by Miles Copeland, infamous former CIA man and brother of The Police's Stewart. Band and label fell out, and Copeland played hardball, freezing payments owed to the band and legally preventing them from either recording or leaving for another label. I ask Lux if this was the worst time to be in The Cramps.

"Absolutely the worst time. We'd just toured Europe and they made up this stuff about Bryan leaving our band to join a voodoo cult! Crap that we wanted nothing to do with because it wasn't true. That was terrible. And it ended up breaking up that line-up because Bryan couldn't take it anymore. We weren't getting our money... people think we sued them for money, but the only thing we wanted was off the label. We couldn't record and it went on for a long time.

"We learned the lesson about not getting involved with anything like that again. There's plenty of places to record cheaply, so we decided to pay for our own recordings and license records to labels. So that was the lesson — stay away from the music industry."

The Cramps decided all this too late for Bryan Gregory. One day in May 1980, after a Cramps show, Gregory drove away with the band's gear and never came back. "We didn't see him for years after he left," Lux recalls. "Then in the late nineties he got in touch with us again and we were writing letters." The reconciliation was brought to an abrupt end when Gregory died suddenly of a heart attack in January 2001, at the age of just 46. "I enjoyed the first line-up," Lux says, "which a lot of people love because Bryan was in the band. Actually, the Bryan and Nick Knox line-up wasn't the first, but I consider it the first line-up. They're all really great memories. Bryan could just do so many weird things. He was just such a weirdo at first. Later on he became... more of a rock star, unfortunately. But at first he'd go out onstage, fold himself up in the yoga lotus position, and run around on his knees. Then he'd spin around on one knee and jump into the audience, which was so dangerous. He really frightened people. That band was a real four-pronged attack."

Gregory has had many replacements down the years, but the best-known was Kid Congo Powers, who spent time in The Gun Club and Nick Cave's Bad Seeds. Powers has an online journal, in which he says that joining The Cramps was a shock because Lux and Ivy ran such a tight ship. Lux proudly agrees.

"We've heard people say that we're the band that can't play and that our schtick is being amateurish. But that has never been what we are. We always wanted to be a good band that plays powerfully and tight. It's like movies that are labelled as trash — the people who were making those movies thought that they were making really great movies. If someone watching doesn't think so, that's too bad. All of our songs have specific parts and if someone's gonna be in our band they have to play those parts. Before we started a band that's what we thought a band was. We went by the Creedence Clearwater Revival model where there's a perfect lead part for a particular song and that's what gets played, as opposed to some bands who just... *jam*." Lux sneers the word 'jam'. "The idea that it's different every night is boring. You should find the perfect thing and just do it. People who do that jamming stuff, it's just an arty attitude: 'I'm so special that whatever I play people will love.' Anyway, The Gun Club had only played two or three times before we saw Kid play with 'em, and they were amazing."

So you stole their bassist? "Yep. And got rid of the competition in one fell swoop. Heh."

The Cramps got through the early eighties and refused to get bitter about missing the pop boat. They've made 13 albums in the last 26 years, including the definitive 'best of' *Off The Bone* and their most recent, 2004's double CD of rarities and live material, *How To Make A Monster*. More importantly, they've played around the world and spread the word on an aesthetic they invented. In every major city on the planet, and particularly cities where many counter-cultural youth go out to party, there will be a club. It will be called something like Born Bad or It Came From Outer Space or Voodoo Lounge or Untamed Youth. It will play fifties rock'n'roll, sixties punk and kitsch mambopopsleaze, and the boys and girls will be dressed in a magnificent mutant strain of vintage chic and DIY gothic fetish wear. Posters and films of Bettie Page, Mamie Van Doren, Elvis, Russ Meyer and Vampira will provide the visuals, and an atmosphere of pervy innocence will pervade. And the boys and girls, whether they're old enough to know it or not, will be living, in those few hours, in The House The Cramps Built. And I dare say new boys and girls will be doing something similar long after you, I or the Cramps have joined the legions of the undead. How many bands invent an entire culture? "I do totally agree, and I hope that doesn't sound too arrogant." It doesn't, Ivy. It doesn't. "I think it wouldn't exist if we didn't. However, it's been around so long now that some of the later versions are innocent in the sense that they maybe don't know it came directly from us. But without us setting that ball in motion, it wouldn't be around. I'm sure of that."

Is your LA home still a shrine to The Cramps' obsessions?

"Yeah, it is. We had to have some extensive remodelling about 10 years ago, because... it wasn't quite as bad as the guy's house in *American Splendor* where the house is sagging, but it was starting to sag under the weight of paintings and records. So we had to jack the house up and put more posts under the floor. There's a lot of leopard-skin. We've got a very Polynesian thing going on."

It's tempting to conclude that The Cramps are pioneers of 'the trash aesthetic'. But our perfect couple don't see it that way. Take it away, Lux: "People will never understand the blues. And they understand it less today than they did back then. Even black people today, a lot of them disown the blues. When people say trash, they're saying that they think the blues is trash, because that's all rock'n'roll is. When people say trash they mean you're not doing something like Pink Floyd. You know, *good music*. It's probably worse here in America than it is over in Europe for people understanding what rock'n'roll is. It's not trash. It's a folk art. Which makes it more important than anything that comes out of a major studio. I'm more interested in Marcel Duchamp taking a bicycle and jamming it in the top of a stool than some artist who's spent his life in front of an easel perfecting his brush-stroke."

Ivy: "For us it was like, the sixties were great — the sixties bands who were influenced by blues and rhythm'n'blues. We loved the early Rolling Stones, The Kinks, Pretty Things, Yardbirds... Later on, it turned from rock'n'roll to rock music — the more progressive, suburban, and more commercial thing. It seems a lot of that is revered now. We loved Led Zeppelin, but we also knew the blues music that it came from. Now people only go as far back as Zeppelin... even Aerosmith." She can't resist a dismissive snort. "So everything's just watered down. What Neil Young represented in the seventies was panhandling hippies singing 'Heart Of Gold'. It's just weird. It's confusing to us that there are punk bands who say they're influenced by Stevie Nicks! Ha! What the hell?"

Lux: "I think it would be great if we were considered the band that made people pay attention to the past again. The blues is something different from other music. It's the music of real crazy people, and it's different from popular music. Sometimes it *becomes* popular music, but it's a whole different thing. And the thing with those old movies and Bettie Page and custom car culture... I think we had a lot to do with making people pay attention to that. And once they pay attention they realise that that's not something to be thrown away and forgotten about. We made people turn around and think about where things came from."

Our time with The Greatest Living Rock'n'Roll Band is coming to an end. There's just time to ask about some of the curious byways of Crampsworld, of which there are many. For example, in the build-up to this feature, *The Stool Pigeon*'s esteemed editor travelled to see The Cramps in Norway. Your correspondent received a delighted text: "Cramps brilliant, as always. Lux got his dick out, as always." Indeed, Lux is probably second only to Iggy Pop — with whom The Cramps have toured and collaborated — in terms of rock penis sightings. Does

Ivy ever say, "Oh, put it away!?"

"No," Lux drawls. "Only when the cops are at the show. Then she'll say, 'Don't do anything tonight. Those cops don't look friendly.' But no, it's really not a part of the show. It just happens sometimes, 'cos... I don't want that to be part of the show. We're not Marilyn Manson or one of those bands who are there to shock people. That's not our main message."

How did you end up doing a song for the *SpongeBob SquarePants* cartoon? Lux: "Our nextdoor neighbour does the background artwork. And he just came by and said, 'I've told my boss that we live next-door and he asked if you would do a song for us.' That simple. It was a lot of fun."

Lux, is it true that all the screams in Francis Ford Coppola's version of *Dracula* are you? "Well, not all of them. We did go to his house and record me screaming, sobbing and sighing for three hours. But I don't think all the screams are me. Sofia Coppola is a really big Cramps fan and came up with the idea: 'Daddy, The Cramps would do a beautiful job.' We've been around long enough now that the little monsters who came to see us when we started out are now in positions of power. It's a wonderful thing that these people come to us."

Nonetheless, you have no major hits and have remained resolutely cultish. Have you ever got disillusioned, and wanted to give up? Ivy: "No. Because we really love playing, we love writing songs, and I love playing guitar. It is hard work doing gigs but we're outside the music business so we don't have all that dispiriting crap to put up with. As far as income, we've done quite well. You can look at it and say, 'We deserve more,' or you can look at all the bands who crashed and burned and didn't get what they were entitled to and say we did really well. We're paid well for gigs and we have a couple of songs in commercials which are very lucrative. There's one in a Cadillac commercial at the moment. We do well enough that this has been worth doing in every possible way. We do what we love for a living and live a good life. Some people go on about having a big house... but Lux and I are both psychic, so that would just frighten us, 'cos all those empty rooms would be full of ghosts. Maybe it's because of our awareness of musical history that we're aware there are so many unsung heroes who never got anything, and we're sure doing better than them. Entitlement is a stoopid thing for anyone to feel."

That's what makes you different from the Ramones. They were desperate for that big hit.

"They stuck together when they hated each other."

The Cramps never seemed like that.

"It'll cost you your life. It'll eat you up, and to not realise that is just deadly. And... they're dead."

If I had to pinpoint a single thing that makes me admire Lux Interior and Poison Ivy Rorschach as much as any living rock band, it's the idea that two ordinary kids could, and did, create an entire self-contained world out of nothing more than music, movies, clothes, working-class history and... love. Big, romantic, lustful, lifelong love for each other and for the things they both adore.

Ivy, you live on Planet Cramps, a fantasy world that you made into a reality, don't you?

"We do. And thank you for understanding that, because some people think it's a band with a career. It's not. It's our life. It's about the right company and creating an atmosphere. It makes us happy but it also promotes creativity and... *vision*. It keeps us free."

GRACE UNDER PRESSURE

"I'm allowed to fuck your brain. Okay?"
The Stool Pigeon Interview with Grace Jones.

By JOHN DORAN
From issue 19, December 2008

At the start of the recording of this phone interview with Grace Jones, while I'm waiting for someone to pick up the receiver, I appear to be breathing really heavily, like someone who is anticipating a very stressful experience. I sound like an astronaut waiting for blast off or a bomb detonation expert who is about to sever the blue wire with a pair of nail cutters. This is perhaps not unsurprising if you look at the popular perception of Grace Jones. She is often seen as a difficult interviewee, probably because of her extraordinary outburst on *The Russell Harty Show* in 1981 when she rained down blows on the hapless talk show host. To me, that has always said more about how shit television was in the eighties than anything else. Who thought it was a good idea to have two guests and a chat show host all sitting in a row, necessitating Harty to turn his back on Jones who responded in a very physical and demonstrative manner? Perhaps she still retains an aura of the 'man eater' that would worry some. One of the more colourful stories that has attached itself to her is the idea that she and Dolph Lundgren used to attack each other with baseball bats as part of their pre-sex rituals. However, that has no bearing on my laboured breathing. Really, it's purely because she's an artist of such standing that I'm bricking it. I probably haven't been this afraid since I interviewed Mark E. Smith.

Now, this attitude will either elicit nods of recognition or howls of derision. She was treated with great mistrust by many in punk circles; seen as a dilettante. The anyone-can-do-it, DIY attitude applied to men with guitars! Not to women! Certainly not to black supermodels! It was as if the sublime deterritorialisation of punk, as predicted by Gilles Deleuze and Fêlix Guattari in their book *Anti-Oedipus: Capitalism and*

Schizophrenia, only lasted for a few years or even just a few months before attitudes were reterritorialised into new lumpen and boring orthodoxies of what was real and acceptable. How quickly they forgot that they were the ones being lambasted by rock critics and prog rock bores just months beforehand for not being 'proper' musicians. Some (but by no means all) punks saw her as the enemy because she was fake and pop. But sonically, her experiments with disco were more radical than Gang of Four's, and her experiments with reggae much more satisfying than those of the Clash.

It was perhaps natural that Grace would grow up an outsider. She was born at some point about six decades ago in Spanish Town, Jamaica into a deeply religious and conservative family (no one seems to know her exact birthday). The immediate family moved to Syracuse, upstate New York when she was a teen and she eventually ran away from home to study drama. Perhaps not unreasonably, she came to the conclusion that her look and accent were too strong for the US, so she moved to Paris where she became a successful model, appearing on the cover of *Vogue*. In 1977, the far-sighted fashion guru Issey Miyake persuaded her that she should combine two of her passions — music and fashion — and this led to a record deal with Island. After some decent enough pop fare that included the singles 'La Vie En Rose' and 'I Need A Man', she began to realise her true potential when she become embroiled in the New York City disco scene, combining threads of reggae, disco, post punk and synth pop into a sublime whole on the albums *Warm Leatherette* and *Nightclubbing*. She released notable collaborations with both Trevor Horn and Nile Rogers in the eighties, but after a long and baffling absence from major musical projects she has recently made an undisputed return to form in the shape of her new album *Hurricane*, which sees her team up with trusted old allies (Sly Dunbar and Robbie Shakespeare) and some new ones (Brian Eno).

The phone keeps on ringing and outside the window the full moon is massive and bright. After an aeon of heavy breathing, a button is pushed and a rich, female accent that is simultaneously French, Jamaican,

American and English says: "...I just hope he's intelligent, that's all I have to say. Whoops! Did you hear me?"

"No," I lie.

"Good!" she roars [not for the last time].

THE STOOL PIGEON: How are you?

GRACE JONES: I am lovely. As well as can be expected when the full moon is coming out.

SP: It's my pleasure to talk to you on the eve of the release of your new album, *Hurricane*. Why haven't we heard from you musically for so long?

GJ: How long are you talking about?

SP: Well, I know you had a single out but I'm talking albums. And you haven't had an album out for 19 years by my count.

GJ: Ah, I see. Album-wise it has been a while. Music-wise it has always been there.

SP: You've been doing musicals and singing on stage as well as the singles, but what prompted you to record a new album?

GJ: It was an accident, actually. Excuse me, I have a lot of movers in my flat at the moment and I'm trying to find somewhere where we can talk quietly. I'm in my new flat in London and I'm having my furniture moved out of storage. Okay, hello John! Actually, it wasn't really an accident. Ivor Guest (producer and on/off boyfriend) was searching for me because he wanted to add my voice to a project that he was doing called *Biomechanics*. He had a wonderful track and I'm always writing lyrics and not thinking whether or not the melody is going to follow, but the melody did fit perfectly with the track and that's how it started; that was the jump start. You must forgive me, I was up until seven this morning editing photos with Chris Cunningham. He is involved in a visual way and also experimenting with his visuals in a musical way. Do you like Chris Cunningham?

SP: A lot.

GJ: Well, we've been working together and I'm just a bit hmmpfff, hmmpff... exhausted! But in a very good way! I'm just making excuses in case I sound a bit... euphoric!

SP: You've always been a night person, haven't you?

GJ: Morning and night actually. I love both extremes. I like working until the morning, so I can see the day and then I like to go to sleep and then get up before sunset. But I love the energy of the morning.

SP: What was it like hooking up with Sly and Robbie again?

GJ: It was as if we'd never been apart. It could be something to do with space between albums as well; I just wanted to work with them again. I did start doing an album with them before — about three tracks — but I didn't get them together playing organically, and I didn't like the outcome of it. And that was one of the reasons why I never released what we did. Some of the songs were already there — one third, let's say — and then this time it really flowed well. It flowed like a river. It really felt right, especially on the track 'Devil In My Life'. The more you listen to it, the deeper it will take you. It has the big symphonic sound that we got at Abbey Road with a big orchestra, which was amazing.

SP: It's quite striking how modern the album sounds, but there's also a direct sonic link to *Warm Leatherette* and *Nightclubbing*.

GJ: That was the purpose. It was a conscious decision to have stuff from the classics... They have become classics, apparently, and I'm just finding that out myself. They have a timeless sound and I love that, really; I love the way they sound, and Ivor who produced the record absolutely loved those records as well. So it seemed like both of our ideas came together at the same time. It was supposed to sound modern and, at the same time, have no time. Sly and Robbie: their sounds have no time. When we work together we make up a sound that will always be new.

70

SP: It's certainly the case that a lot of bands are influenced by you and the period that spawned you; that of post punk. Many bands look up to Joy Division, Tom Tom Club, Wire... But does this go both ways? Do you keep up with modern music?

GJ: I do and I don't. I keep up with music. Sometimes some friends will play me Captain Beefheart and then I will listen to some modern stuff. For me, though, I think that Captain Beefheart will always be modern. And Tom Waits will always be modern. He makes a poetry that will always be married to melodies that are unique. This combination for me is always modern. I guess I'm trying to say that trends — when you have one hit and then everyone wants to sound like that one hit, and people tend to do that, going, 'Oh, this is a hit so let's make everything for the next 10 years sound like that' — drive me totally mad.

SP: The trouble with the major labels now is that as soon as something becomes fashionable, they jump on it with all the money instead of allowing artists to develop.

GJ: I'm happy that you see that. Not many people see that. But it's happening in many ways, and not just in record companies. This sort of thing happens in everything — politics, for example. I guess I'm just totally anti the whole system that you have to get caught up into. You end up with no choice left to you anymore.

SP: Do you think it's harder to be a creative person in 2008 than it was in 1978?

GJ: No, never. It's not harder. One just has to do it. That is all. Whatever one is creating, one has to stick to one's guns and just do it. That is all. Put your foot down and do not let your work be compromised.

SP: You've studied theatre and been in films and, according to an interview I was reading recently, you were a self-confessed 'art groupie'...

71

GJ: That's a song, actually. 'Art Groupie' off *Warm Leatherette* [it's actually off *Nightclubbing*]. That is one of my favourites.

SP: I know the song. I suppose what I'm driving at is that in every aspect of your life you appear to be creative, whether it is music, fashion, or art. Is this a compulsion?

GJ: I think it's just me. It is me. It's not 100 per cent me, but it's definitely in my dreams and imagination. It is a big part of me. My dreams and imagination.

SP: With *Hurricane*, it seems to me to be a very sensual record; very grounded in the physical. Even if you just look at the titles: 'William's Blood', 'I'm Crying', 'Sunset Sunrise'...

GJ: Of course it's sensual. All emotions are sensual. It goes from one extreme to another. They are all sensual emotions. Even if I sing like a robot, it is still an emotional robot. Do you know what I mean?

SP: I do and I think there is a certain way of singing that I think you and certain other artists used that may have ostensibly been judged as slightly robotic, but was essentially very soulful.

GJ: Well, it's got to come from the soul. Where else is it going to come from? Some songs come from my head, some from my throat, but there will always be moments when it is an injection of the soul.

SP: Tell us about your childhood in Jamaica. What were you like as a school child?

GJ: Competitive. Sporty. I think religion played a big part of it. My granduncle ruled, in Pentecostal rules. He was the Bishop of Jamaica. I think that is already out there somewhere! I'm telling you this so you will get a feeling for how this affected me. Because of this, I was very sporty and competitive. It was also a combination of having three brothers and a sister who lived round the corner. My step-grandfather was an elder in the church of my grandmother's brother, with my granduncle, who was the Bishop. So it was a lot of discipline. You have to know what you're going to be from the age of eight, for example.

SP: How did you see your life panning out when you were that age?

GJ: The plan was to be baptised and receive the Holy Ghost and go to study as a school teacher. And somewhere in this plan there were languages as well. I wanted to teach many different languages, so that meant lots of travel. Books? Okay. But travel was better for learning languages. That's what I dreamt of. When I was young I would see a jungle — not a real jungle but some trees when I was going to the shop to get milk — and in those trees I would see lions and tigers and bears. And I guess this had a lot to do with the fantasies of travel that I had when I was a child.

SP: Did you suffer culture shock when you moved to Syracuse?

GJ: Absolutely! But in the best way. I had never seen snow before! And I'm still shocked every time I see snow. The first bit of snow each year... I stay up and I watch it. And then I go out and pick it up and eat it and move around in it. That is culture shock alright [starts howling with laughter].

SP: Apart from the weather...

GJ: [whispering] I wish you were here.

SP: I wish I was. It sounds like a good laugh.

GJ: [more laughter and squealing] It is.

SP: What did people make of you?

GJ: Well, everyone thought I was brilliant. It was a technical thing [bursts into laughter]. Oh my God! Right, in Jamaica we had the English way of schooling from the age of four, so when I got to America I was already a few years advanced because I started school at the age of three-and-a-half rather than six and my grades moved up accordingly.

In America, they start you at school at six because the grades are different. I had to take a test and they didn't know what to do with me. It wasn't that I was any smarter; I had just started younger. All of a sudden I was jumped from eighth to tenth grade. They said I was very smart, but I was only smart in languages, really. Cooking was a disaster! But I am learning now. I have seven meals for each seven days of the week.

SP: What is the best dish that you cook?
GJ: Carbonara. Arrabiata. Mmmmmm!

SP: Nice and spicy.
GJ: Uh huhhhh. Breaded rack of lamb. Jamaican country chicken. Jamaican curry chicken. Oooh la la la! And grilled steaks or lamb chops, and that's it.

SP: When you moved to Syracuse, did you rebel against your family's religion?
GJ: I left as quickly as I could. You can't rebel more than that. I just disappeared. I went to do plays after leaving school. There were nine of us — The Ruskin Players — and we did Shakespeare and the classics. I did that for one year and then I didn't come home. They knew where I was, but they didn't know how to find me.

SP: Right.
GJ: You don't understand what I meant by that, do you?

SP: Not entirely.
GJ: I sent them letters, of course. But the letters said I was upstairs when I was downstairs.

SP: Ah.
GJ: It's the bloody truth. I have no idea how you are going to write it! I'm sorry.

SP: Don't be, it's interesting.

GJ: Well, you keep some of it for yourself. You promise?

SP: I will do.

GJ: Good. We can do something later...

SP: In some senses, you were quite rebellious then?

GJ: I was totally rebellious. That's what I mean about disappearing. I changed my name. I became a go-go dancer. For theatrical reasons, of course. I was 15 or 16. I would be locked up now. Being 15 and doing that is illegal.

SP: Do you think that people don't know how to deal with wilful or autonomous teenage girls?

GJ: People? People in general? Are you talking about me being 15? I was like a runaway, but I wasn't a runaway — I was in the middle because I was working. After the work was done, you know, then I disappeared letting them know that I was okay. So there is a difference between that and completely disappearing and not letting anyone know where you are. I let them know I was okay. And then I showed up on a motorcycle. Wearing hippy beads. On acid.

SP: You were a hippy?

GJ: I was a wannabe hippy. I guess I still had the religion in me, but I got as close as I thought I could.

SP: How did you get on with LSD?

GJ: I loved it. But I only took it for therapeutic reasons. I wouldn't do it anymore because, you know, I had the best. I had it from the *doctors*.

SP: The doctor prescribed it to you!?

GJ: No! The witch doctor!

SP: Ah, I see. I was going to say...

GJ: Oh, do come on! It is different now. In that time, it was under someone who helped you through it if you were going to have a bad time, or talked you through in different directions. I didn't know that, though. I just opened my mouth and swallowed. But I was lucky.

SP: I do think it's helpful to take it a few times when you're younger. It can help you see different possibilities.

GJ: Yeah, but you can also kill yourself. Or you can learn. Again, I did it under very good supervision. And there is a time for everything. There is a time to take it and a time not to take it. You shouldn't take it when you're feeling bad. You have to take it when you are feeling good. And that applies to every drug.

SP: When was the last time you took drugs?

GJ: I just had a joint while I was talking to you then.

SP: Oh right! Was it nice?

GJ: Well, it's heavy. I was having stress and I don't like having prescription drugs. Arghhhh! That shouldn't even come out of my mouth! I hate prescription drugs! They don't tell you everything that is in them.

SP: Speaking as a mother, what is your position on drugs when people ask you about them?

GJ: I always say, 'Prescription drugs can be even worse than illegal drugs. The only difference is the legality.' I'm running for president, what can I tell you! I've lived long enough to feel the sway of corporations both legal and illegal. Corporations give you drugs and they prescribe and prescribe them and they can be worse for you. Whereas you have illegal drugs and that is all about moderation. You have to know your body. It is like an allergy. Some people can have an allergy to feathers, so you don't buy a pillow with feathers, right? But, at the same time, someone can cure their eyesight by smoking a little bit of marijuana. Who is to say which should be illegal: the pillow that you

76

might be allergic to or the marijuana tea that might cure your eyesight? Who is making those decisions? The individual has to do it. You get a reaction immediately the first time you use it. If you have a cigarette for the first time, you cough and that means your body doesn't like it. I smoke once in a while. The first cough I get I put it down. Cigarettes are legal though, right? They are the biggest motherfucking killers in the fucking world, right? I have a very good friend who can't stop. They can stop heroin. They can stop coke. They can stop sex. But, hello! HELLO!? They can't stop smoking. What does that tell you? Everything in moderation and know your own body. Keep on following the yellow brick road.

SP: Talking of following roads, how did you come to move to France?

GJ: That was for my modelling career and I just wanted to travel. I just wanted to travel. I knew that my Jamaican accent wasn't going to get me any work so I went to Europe and hitchhiked from Luxembourg to Paris. I stood on the wrong side of the road! Somebody stopped and told me. I remember getting the train some of the way sitting on the floor of the carriage with these people playing guitars. That was when the record deal thing happened for the first time. I was with Issey Miyake, who was very important in my career, because he introduced the modelling and singing together with my first record, 'I Need A Man'. And I love him for that. That allowed me to... he saw something in me that I couldn't see in myself. I was modelling to pay my rent, but he said I should combine the modelling and the singing. So I combine everything now!

SP: What was your version of 'Imagine' like?

GJ: 'Imagine'? You know what? I think it is recorded somewhere. But it was one of the songs... Wait! How do you know about that!? How do you know!?

SP: Ah ha, I've been doing my research!

GJ: Oh God, you're good. You are very good. I like that. Hmmmmm!

SP: Ha ha! Well, I believe you did 'Imagine' and 'Dirty Old Man'?

GJ: Yeah, but 'Imagine' was my absolute favourite. Shall I sing it for you?

SP: Oh yeah, that would be great.

GJ: [Sings 'Imagine'.] I still love that song and maybe I will cover it again. But back then I sang it terribly. I was so nervous.

SP: I believe you took singing lessons after that, but you didn't react very well to your teacher.

GJ: Not the French one. My French singing teacher was like Hitler. Oh God, you are laughing. Are you German?

SP: No, I'm from Liverpool. I just thought it was a funny description.

GJ: He was a fucking character. I thought you must have been from Germany.

SP: No, I'm from Liverpool.

GJ: I love Liverpool! Now I definitely have to meet you. I'm lighting a cigarette. Please hold on Mr Liverpool. We have 15 minutes and then there is another call, but don't worry, 15 minutes is a long time.

SP: Er, it certainly is. What did you get from singing lessons?

GJ: I'll give you an example, okay? I went to sing with Pavarotti, which was for me the height of my vocal achievement. Now, my attitude had always been, 'Meh.' Rock'n'roll mixed with a little bit of church; hit that note if you can and, if you can't, rap it. But with Pavarotti I wanted to hit the highest highs with him. I went to Venice and I did a crash course in operatics and the voice. After two weeks, I went out saying I couldn't stand it anymore. I said tonight I'm going to drink spirits and smoke as many cigarettes as I can and go into my singing lesson tomorrow and see what has happened to my voice. I lost four notes on the scale of the piano, and that was when I learned about my voice. For some people, they can do that and it won't affect them, but for me I lost the ability to hit those notes. I knew that affected me in a way that it doesn't affect anyone else. The voice is a unique thing. Some people can get totally, totally high and sing the note on a dime, but my voice doesn't do that.

SP: When did you first become aware of disco music?

GJ: I was a dancing disco queen and disco was the best to dance to. It was an accumulation of the time and the sound system had a lot to do with it. It was very church, to be honest. My upbringing in the church had a lot to do with it. Disco was like the celebration of music through dance and — my God! — when you heard the music sometimes it was like, 'If you don't get up and dance, you aren't human!'

SP: It's interesting that you have links to both 'pure' disco and the post punk/alternative strands of disco. Not many other artists do.

GJ: It is experience, dear. I experienced the best of disco in the late seventies. But that was only its name then. The name changes. Dance has always existed and disco really existed before that period and then after as well. Disco existed before we were all born and will exist afterwards. It is a ritual — it is a celebration — and it is the same kind of music that we call disco or rock'n'roll or a whole list of names that we can call it. Call it what you will, nothing will change the fact that certain kinds of music will make you want to celebrate or party. I love house! I love house music!

SP: When you were younger, you had a reputation as a 'wilful' model who perhaps lost out on some jobs because you would just shave your own hair off. You certainly had a reputation as a model who wasn't going to be pushed around. What do you think when you see lots and lots of younger models starving themselves down to a size zero?

GJ: Well, I certainly wasn't going to play by the rules. Actually, I didn't know there were any rules. When you start in that business the rules are imposed upon you, but when you stay in the business long enough the rules could be broken. A face could break the rules. Meaning: 'You've got that face, we don't care what your body looks like.' They don't do that anymore. It's a power thing. It's a control thing. The designers make the samples of the clothes to fit that size zero, so when they call you in for a cattle call, it's going to be whoever fits this size is going to be the one who stands a chance of being picked. And I've got a problem with that. It's corporate cannibal. I understand it, but I don't like it. I understand it because I had to be measured from head-to-toe, and to stand on tip-toes to get into the top model agencies. I did a little bit of cheating, but once I got in the door I broke the door down. I didn't know I was breaking the door down until after I did it, and then they said, 'You broke the bloody door down!'

SP: Presumably you have another single coming off the album?

GJ: Yeah. 'William's Blood'.

SP: How are we doing for time?

GJ: I don't know, honey... I'm just here!

SP: Well, I'm going to keep on asking questions until someone asks me to stop.

GJ: [roars laughing] Why don't you come for dinner?

SP: [nervously] Why don't I come for dinner? That's a good question.

GJ: What do you like to eat?

SP: Pasta.

GJ: Pasta. Oooh la la. Okay, I can do that.

SP: Ah. Right. I'm all flustered now. My mind's gone blank.
GJ: [purrs] Oh, don't get all flustered.

SP: Er, what's it like working with Brian Eno?
GJ: Brian and I have always passed like ships in the night. I've known him for years but never really met him. You know, that kind of thing.

SP: You seem like an ideal pairing.
GJ: I know! We knew each other but never met each other. Well, I met him at a documentary screening and he wanted me to sing this gospel song for him and it just jumped into my head that we should work together. I asked him if he would want to work on the project and he said, 'I don't want to produce! I don't want to produce! I just want to be one of the musicians and have some fun.' And I said, 'That's okay by me.'

SP: You do have a knack for working with good people.
GJ: It's not just a knack. They're people that I meet on the yellow brick road.

SP: Where do you think that the yellow brick road will take you in the next few years?
GJ: I don't know what I'm going to be doing in two years or even in two weeks. I have to live for today.

SP: Well, that's a great answer and thank you very much for talking to me.
GJ: How do I meet you? I like you very much.

SP: Miss Jones! You are naughty...
GJ: Well, it has nothing to do with naughty. I like your brain. I'm

allowed to fuck your brain. Okay? I like your brain, that is all, and I think we should meet.

SP: The very second I hang up, I'll pass on all of my contact details to the PR woman.

GJ: No, give them to me. There are too many people sometimes.

SP: Do you have a pen?

GJ: I have it here in my hand. It is red. I'm trying to write it on the bed but it keeps on sinking into the mattress. Hmmm mmmmm!

SP: Oh, Miss Jones!

WIDE AWAKE

The family-like music scene in Omaha, Nebraska that Bright Eyes and Tilly And The Wall drew attention to remains an ideal, and it's still producing amazing new bands.

By Emma-Lee Moss

From issue 11, May 2007

When you're with Lightspeed Champion, it's always about MySpace. "I'm alternating between accounts right now," he explains, not looking up to witness his debut album being edited. In the last hour, he has re-configured his top 20 twice, first by aesthetic, then in order of righteousness. The latter system means I have finally beaten The Strokes. At last look, Fatty Casablancas and Co. are lagging behind me by two places and I'm sitting pretty on row one between Semifinalists and some dude called Train Chronicles. I guess you can sell a million records and grace the cover of *Rolling Stone*, but until you've waited eight hours at Chicago Airport en route to Omaha, where you're booked to sing "shoop shoops" on Dev's album, you're nothing but a fourth row nobody. People have to scroll down to see you.

Look outside the window and the world is awesome. Buried under two feet of snow are the kind of cars they drive in indie films about people who can't get dates and love comics; the kind you drive to the side of a known beauty spot and make out in, or drink your keg out of, or drive home to mom and dad after the prom, bummed out because some girl killed everyone with her telekinetic powers. On one side of the courtyard resides Mike Mogis, Bright Eyes producer and founder of Saddle Creek Records; on the other side is Conor Oberst's house, or Conor to those who think that knowing where he lives is enough. Somewhere in between are the studio we're recording in and a four-bedroom house for travelling bands. It's called the Frat House.

"We had Mates Of State living here for a while," remembers Ian, Mike's engineer and all round big brother type. "They just showed up, but I don't remember why..."

Ian's quite blasé about bands that make me squeal with joy. I guess when Conor Oberst's garden is where you keep your sledge, and Tim Kasher from Cursive is the guy who got your car out of the snow this morning, you don't really care what Mates Of State are doing in your studio. They just showed up. Meh, it's just Mates Of State. Indeed, I've been here for two days and I'm also getting kind of blasé. Hanging around at the mall we see The Faint's drummer four times; I'm pretty sure I played Xbox with the guy from Two Gallants; and, if I wanted to, I could get a coffee from Tilly And The Wall's Jamie Pressnall, who supplements the income she receives from tap-dancing by working as a barista at Caffeine Dreams. It seems that every corner of Omaha is peppered with a little piece of cult history, hidden among the normals in their Hilfiger jeans and snow boots. I wonder if any of the kids who wake up to Neely Jenkins as a substitute teacher realise that she is one of the most loved musicians in Omaha? It's like Graham Coxon walking into maths class and scrawling his name across the board.

If you want to look at homegrown successes, Tilly And The Wall are a good place to start. Tap-dancer Jamie and singer Neely were in Conor's high school band Park Ave., whose sweet, lo-fi sensibilities could be considered a prototype for the Saddle Creek sound. Kianna Alarid, singer and chanter, was also in a high school band, with members of The Faint, and later sang for Rilo Kiley. As for the two boys, Derek and Nick, they made their way to Omaha in the fall of 2001, lured by a friend who was playing in... Bright Eyes.

"We were really lucky to have friends who supported us from the beginning," says Kianna. "Put it this way: our first tour was with Bright Eyes; our second tour was with Bright Eyes; and our third tour was with Rilo Kiley. We were just given the opportunity to reach people of a similar audience, and they responded."

"We did try to send CDs out before Conor came along," adds Neely, "but people would just poop on them and send them back."

It just goes to show what a little nurturing can do. Born out of a tight community and the belief of a few friends, Tilly have gone on to make a bigger impact in the UK than most of their senior counter-parts. Four years after Conor created Team Love just to sign them, their presence over here has refocused the spotlight on Omaha, and Jamie is the first Nebraskan to appear on the all-knowing, definitive, life changing, er, *NME* cool list. More importantly, when the culture board decided to honour local music with the Omaha Music Awards, Tilly And The Wall were the only band on TV that didn't make Steps look classy.

"I guess you could call us Jesus freaks," declared a member of Christian metal band Stigmata, "'cause we love Jesus, and we're *freaks*!" Covered entirely in white paint and bald as the day he was born, the man doesn't make a great spokesman for the rest of Omaha. Actually neither does the presenter, who asks Jamie why she tap-dances and thanks her before she answers. The last shot of the evening is Derek dissolving into giggles on the edge of the screen.

"It was like high school," he laughs, "but it was cool that they tried..."

Sitting around the Frat House table watching Tilly on the television and drinking beer with Derek, Kianna and their friends, it doesn't seem like there's anything outside of this perfect microcosm. Even on our epic evening out, where we take in an arcade and a bowling alley untouched since the fifties, everything seems like incidental scenery in an unwritten biography — the story of what happens next. And what will happen? The new wave of bands, who I meet while bowling, and who mainly bowl like little girls, seem ready to break into the spotlight pretty soon. There's the Family Radio, fronted by the singer from Son, Ambulance; Flowers Forever, Derek's solo project; and Coyote Bones, whose singer David followed the Tilly boys from Atlanta. In the same way that the early Omaha bands shared a vision of sound, this new gang are united by a bright, raucous pop aesthetic, the natural evolution from the bands they follow, whose legacy they arrived to make use of.

"Saddle Creek created a foundation for us to get heard," says David. "People trust the scene over here, so we get a head start."

Included in the legacy is the notion of self-sufficiency. Everybody in David's circle are able to record and release their material off their own back, be it in his basement, on downtime in Mike's studio, through Saddle Creek or any of the myriad labels following in its wake. There's even an on-hand video director, Nik, whose weird, colourful films will one day form a visual reference for the scene. The week after I leave, he makes a Coyote Bones video in the famous basement. The footage of boys and girls in sombreros and giant sunglasses looks pretty low budget, and the scrappiness is enhanced by Dev falling over and David dropping his bunny ears mid-chorus, but it looks exactly how it should. It's just a group of friends in the midst of the best party ever, and should they wake up in an alternate universe where they're bankers and car dealers, it will exist as a recorded reminder of a moment in time. The three of us from England also have a record of when we crashed that party — a cover of Phantom Planet's 'California' sung at midnight around a wind-up melodica, the lyrics changed to 'Oh Nebraska, here we come…'

While we're drinking around the TV, I hear the name Simon Joyner mentioned. A month later, at Tilly's sold-out Scala show in London, Derek brings him up again.

"He was really big in Omaha," he tells me, "Conor just loved him and he looked to him for inspiration. He was the best singer-songwriter…"

Later that afternoon, I email a friend who's cooler than me.

"Simon Joyner?" I ask him.

Five minutes later the reply comes. "*A necessity*," it reads, and so I hit the MySpace angle again. It seems that even obscure folk artists who exist wilfully below the radar are capable of being online and I find myself, on a spring day in Camden, reintroduced to the vast bleakness of Omaha on a pair of computer speakers.

If there was ever a soundtrack to the Omaha that I saw, this music would be it. Some of his songs are for walking through snowdrifts to the mall, surrounded by neon signs and miles and miles of road. Some songs are for when the snow subsides, and you are navigating backyards to look through someone's window. And some songs are for the large stretches of park that I glimpsed through the glass of a 4x4 — songs that started their life on a scrap of floor at Kilgore's, the legendary Omaha café where Joyner, Conor and most of the early songwriters started out.

"It was sort of a songwriting competition every Thursday night, each of us trying to outdo each other," says Joyner of the early days. "It was a pretty popular thing and I cut my teeth on that regular gig. Kilgore's kind of became a kind of revolving door for Omaha songwriters wood-shedding and developing."

Having met Conor at one of these events, Joyner and his friends helped to put out his first tape, a split with Bill Hoover called *Kill The Monster Before It Eats Baby*. However, it wasn't just in enterprise that Joyner's influence can be seen. If you listen to his recordings and compare them with early Bright Eyes, it's easy to see how 14-year-old Conor was affected by their association. They're lo-fi, wordy, lightly tinged with a countrified melancholy, and narrated primarily through the eyes of one sexually charged, geeky adolescent 'I'.

I was drunk, I didn't let on
As I stood before your door at dawn
Guess I might have awakened the dogs
'Cause the shadows started coughing them out
So I put my hands into my hair
And I pulled and let it hurt
There's a light going out somewhere
Thought I could hear it through the woods

So he sings on 'One For The Catholic Girls', and you can just imagine Conor listening to this through an old cassette deck and thinking, "This is how music is supposed to sound."

If Joyner acknowledges his part in the birth of the Omaha sound, he doesn't mention it. He does, however, shed some light on how he separated from the others, purposefully sticking to the shadows while they rocketed onto the world stage.

"All those guys were friends who went to the same school and lived in the same neighbourhood," he says. "It was a tight clique, so it made sense for them to start a label devoted to championing their music. I was more of a downtown person and a product of a broken home and the public school system. All those guys are recovering Jesuits — frustrated Catholic kids from another part of town with a slightly different upbringing. Our scenes were certainly different, but I loved them and their energy and I loved that they all stuck together and supported each other. It's been that way ever since. Amazing devotion. And once they started performing and recording, we've supported one another, performing and recording together. It's very Midwestern, this Omaha sound, and by that I mean there is smalltown loyalty and support and everyone is very polite. We're all ambitious in our own ways, but not at the expense of one another. It really is a lot like a family dynamic when I think about it."

One last member of this family to include is David Dondero, who I meet in Edinburgh. By some coincidence, he is playing down the road from Tilly while we're on tour and we arrive in some stinking old man's pub just in time to see him quietly pack his guitar away mid-song and walk out. I don't see him in Omaha, and I'm not sure that he lives there, but in my head he belongs with the others, in a mythological smalltown littered with fast food outlets and gas stations, where the only way out is to sing.

It's two months later and the Lightspeed Champion record is mixed, mastered and packed neatly into little plastic sleeves. We go to watch Bright Eyes play Koko in London, standing with our arms crossed in what I hope is a 'we know them' pose. At one point Mike turns on the distortion pedal.

"That is *so* Mike," I say.

"Totally," sighs Dev.

When I get home I tell my flatmate, "I think we should start a scene. Be a bit more like a family."

"Okay," he agrees, climbing down the stairs. We sit in silence for 10 minutes.

"I wish you were Bright Eyes," I tell him.

"I wish you were dead," he replies, and walks out.

Later, in bed, I resolve to take him out of my top friends and plot my route back to Omaha. Until Graham Coxon *walks into my house* and asks to borrow a snow blower, this town is dead to me.

BUCK RIGHT OFF

Bradford Cox of Deerhunter would rather you didn't stalk him.

By ALEX MARSHALL
From issue 18, October 2008

Almost a year ago to the day, I had the pleasure of interviewing Bradford Cox, frontman of Atlanta's finest, Deerhunter. It was a pleasure for all of three questions. After a few words about their then new album *Cryptograms*, he spent the next half-hour listing his personal problems. He spoke about the anti-depressants he was taking, and how those meant he couldn't come; he told me about suffering from Marfans, a syndrome that makes his limbs disproportionately long and has hospitalised him more than once; and he complained that Deerhunter was limiting him musically, and explained why he wanted to write songs without drums or bass.

"Have you told your rhythm section?" I asked.

He didn't laugh.

He was ridiculously self-centred, but it seemed in character. Watching Deerhunter live at the time largely involved gawping at Bradford. He would come on stage in a dress, then spend the opening 10 minutes looping his voice into a drone before the rest of the band joined in. And if you visited their blog? Well, he had a habit of posting dodgy pictures on it.

I gave the group a month. Tops.

Guitarist Colin Mee almost proved me right by leaving shortly afterwards, saying hilariously, about the blog: "I don't want the world to know what our excrement looks like... It's just a way to maintain attention when the music should speak for itself."

A year later and all seems to have changed. Deerhunter's forthcoming new album, *Microcastle*, is a real blinder. Out have gone the six-minute ambient passages and in has come some staggering songwriting: delicate pop songs, tearful campfire singalongs and exhilaratingly loud jams.

And they appear to have become much more of a band. Bradford's voice doesn't dominate the record as it did on *Cryptograms* and the lyrics don't dwell on his past. Guitarist Lockett Pundt even sings its two best songs, and it's the same with them when they play live: Bradford, wearing baggy t-shirts, now spends gigs happily playing guitar, letting the other members share the spotlight.

I pick up the phone expecting to hear a happier Bradford on the other end. A stupid thought. During the course of our half-hour chat, he seems to want to make only two points: one, he writes and records a lot of music and, two, he'd be much happier if people left him to it.

"I don't give a shit who likes us," he says. "In fact, the fewer people who like us, the less I have to leave my room and stop making music."

"All I do is record," he adds later. "It's the only interest I have. At all. I don't need anybody or anything else."

I ask him what's provoked the changes in the band; why he's trying to be less personal. "The reason I was so open in the past is because I didn't know that people were actually paying attention," he says. "So I have taken a rational step back from that. But, look, my problems are internal, and they really aren't that interesting. I mean, everyone's miserable, so why's my misery any more or less interesting than anyone else's? Can't we just talk about the music?"

Deerhunter were formed back in 2001, when Bradford met drummer Moses Archuleta at a show at Atlanta's legendary Alphabet House — a punk girl's bed-sit that occasionally put on gigs. The pair were eventually joined by Colin, who was kipping on the Black Lips' floor at the time, and Justin Bosworth on bass.

According to Moses, they spent the next three years "just having fun, playing with no direction" until 2004 when Justin got killed by a car while skateboarding. Josh Fauver was brought in as a replacement. The debut album that followed, *Turn It Up, Faggot*, is an unsurprisingly nasty listen.

Shortly after that came out, Bradford invited his best friend Lockett to join the band and, after a few more years' hard graft, they released *Cryptograms*. Since that, they've done little but tour the States. *Microcastle* was written in one of the few breaks they've allowed themselves.

I ask Bradford if there was any idea behind the record, because it certainly sounds like they were going for a more immediate sound. "There's no real answer to that," he replies. "I mean there's no developmental process I could explain to you; no ideas behind it. I make music constantly. I could have made five records in between *Cryptograms* and this."

He goes on: "I don't depend on anything for inspiration. I don't have to take drugs to write. I don't have to drink to record. I don't get distracted by pussy or ass — boys and girls or crap on TV. I have a very one-dimensional personality. I'm only interested in music and recording. I am a normal person. I have good relationships with my parents and family. But outside of them, I'm not that interested in people. I mean, I have pals — 'buddies' — but I don't have the romantic or sexual distractions other people have. I don't feel I need to have someone else come into my life and be an inspiration to me. I'm more inspired by anything from girl groups to Rauschenberg collages to Tiffany lamps."

So what inspired *Microcastle*? "Girls groups, Rauschenberg collages and Tiffany lamps," he replies, deadpan.

Bradford mentions his love of girl groups in practically every interview he does, even though you can't hear an ounce of them in Deerhunter's music. Since he sounds miserable already, I decide to tell him that.

"Yes, but I don't like ripping off my influences," he says. "Music doesn't need to be digested a second time and re-shat out. You just lose bulk in the stool then; you get diarrhoea. I'm inspired by the ambience of girl group records — everything from the drums to the way the guitars sound. But I've no interest in copying them. I don't want to sound like them."

After saying this, Bradford starts name-checking his favourite girl groups. He mentions Martha & The Vandellas and The Cookies, and then starts filling me in on who they actually were. And, magically, he's suddenly funny, interesting and opinionated. Everything he wasn't before. It's as if he's trying to prove his point that all he's interested in is music and nothing else.

He goes off on such tangents several times later, too, talking about everyone from Lil' Wayne ("a genius from outer space who just shits out verses") to Jay Reatard (opinions on whom he only gives off the record).

It's not where I wanted the interview to go, but at least it means he's not sounding depressed. Unfortunately, I ruin it by asking what his hopes for *Microcastle* are.

"I don't give a fuck what anyone thinks, really," he says. "At this point in time I really, genuinely, don't care about anyone's opinion. That might change — I'm not a fortune teller — but I'm completely stripped of idealism and ambition right now. I would really like to take a year out in my bedroom, enjoying air conditioning, only going out for food. I mean what do I get from this? Money? Adoration from a group of kids? That's cool, but I don't need it, and it doesn't really change anything. What have I got to be ambitious for? That's a good question."

CHILDBALLADE

*After a decade in the wilderness, during which time it was suspected he may have
been claimed by heroin addiction, Jonathan Fire*Eater's extraordinary frontman
Stewart Lupton is back with a new band.*

By PHIL HEBBLETHWAITE

From issue 12, Summer 2007

Bands that show indescribable promise, deliver on it for a brief moment,
then spectacularly implode are a dime a dozen in rock'n'roll, but few of
their stories are as dramatic, intriguing and, ultimately, tragic as Jonathan
Fire*Eater's. This brilliant group of childhood best friends from New
York, via Washington DC, went from being perhaps the most hyped
American band of the mid-nineties, signing a million dollar contract with
David Geffen's DreamWorks (the label's launch band), being courted to
model for Calvin Klein, then totally self-destructing three years later. It
seems almost impossible to imagine but, according to their publicist at the
time (a former professional dominatrix called Erin Norris), the band held
a meeting before the release of their major label debut, 1997's *Wolf Songs
For Lambs*, to request that sales be halted at 500,000. For a number of
reasons, not only because it was their least immediate recording, it ended
up selling somewhere between 7,000 and 12,000 and has long, long been
out of print. The two records that preceded it, 'The Public Hanging Of A
Movie Star' EP from 1995, and 1996's mini album, *Tremble Under Boom
Lights*, are also lost to time, despite being responsible for all the fuss, and
understandably so: the blueprint for the New York garage rock explosion
that The Strokes would end up leading five years later can be found in
those eight short songs. It's not fair to say The Strokes wholesale ripped
Jonathan Fire*Eater off, but they're indebted and so are the Yeah Yeah
Yeahs and Interpol.

The tragedy in Jonathan Fire*Eater's story concerns their snarling
and literary frontman, Stewart Lupton, the band's bona fide star. Three
other members (organist Walter Martin, guitar player Paul Maroon, and
drummer Matt Barrick) went on to form The Walkmen with Hamilton

Leithauser and Pete Bauer from The Recoys and make a career of music. Stewart, whose on-off battle with heroin was cited as a primary reason for Jonathan Fire*Eater's collapse, performed for a while as Stewart Stephenson with his friend Judah Bauer from the Jon Spencer Blues Explosion, then fell totally off the radar. He quickly turned into a mythologised figure. "Whatever happened to Stewart Lupton?" became an often-posed question in internet fan forums, and with no one able to provide a concrete answer, an appalling rumour began to spread: that addiction had killed him.

Stewart Lupton, though, is not just another example of a super talent who pissed his chance up the wall. Unsurprisingly, when he found out about his supposed demise he plotted something of a comeback. First, he posted a message online saying not only was he alive, he also had a new band together called Childballads. Simultaneously and coincidentally, James Oldham, formerly of the *NME*, huge Jonathan Fire*Eater fan and boss of Loog Records (home of The Horrors, Patrick Wolf and The Bravery) had himself been Googling Stewart's name to try and find out where he was. He stumbled upon the post, tracked him down and suggested putting a Childballads record out. That was 2005, seven years after Jonathan Fire*Eater split. It took till March 2007 for the folksy six-track mini album to arrive and, best of all, it wasn't just good, it was exceptional. "I keep hearing talk of the doom and they're sending the meek home," the title track begins, revealing, "But that ain't half as bad as the shadow that's caught in the hollow of a cheekbone."

Stewart even returned to the UK for the first time in almost a decade, playing an impassioned Childballads show at London's Metro Club on April 30 to a shockingly small number of people (about 30), followed by a Cat Power support slot the day after and a few dates in France. The band have also performed headline gigs in the US and have been guests of Interpol and The Fiery Furnaces. Against all the odds, it seems this most wild and intelligent artist, still only 32, is officially back. He's flat old-fashioned broke and the drugs haven't been left behind yet, but he's giving it another shot and, creatively, he's currently well on top of his game.

That Stewart Lupton could have been as big a star as Julian Casablancas, and still could be, is something for him to muse about and he admits to sometimes doing so. Both exhibit a detached cool on stage and the parallels don't stop there. There are strong similarities in the sounds of Jonathan Fire*Eater and The Strokes and all their members were privately educated. Jonathan Fire*Eater attended St. Alban's School in Washington DC (former Vice President Al Gore, himself a Senator's son, is an alumnus too) before moving to New York where they lived a double life of studying at some of the city's renowned universities and falling over each other in a shit-hole two-bedroom apartment in the then-dangerous Lower East Side. They practised in a boiler room in a basement at Columbia University, where three of the five were students, and it was there that they discovered their sound. When they took it to the clubs, the band, and particularly Stewart, caused near pandemonium. As fans remember it, Stewart would bound on stage after a brief instrumental introduction, then deliver his lyrics with "fever" and a trademark "death grip on the mic stand".

"Right now the record companies are sort of circling like vultures," said Stewart in 1996, soon after the release of *Temple Under Boom Lights*. The three-album million-dollar deal they eventually signed with DreamWorks was an unusual one: they were to keep full creative control and, most brilliantly, their nearly toothless manager was to get a full set of new gnashers. The press enjoyed that far more than the fact they refused to make a video for their debut major-label single and were reluctant to do interviews with magazines they thought were lame. They were accused of arrogance and self-obsession by journalists, who gleefully sharpened their knives to review what would end up becoming their first and only album for DreamWorks. "Loudest buzz, but little real-life bang," the *Los Angeles Times* wrote in December 1997. By July the next year, Jonathan Fire*Eater were over. Distraught and in ill health (he was reported as being "absolutely fucked out of his gourd" during their 11.30am Glastonbury performance that June), Stewart returned home to his parent's house in Washington DC. He certainly hasn't been completely out of it these past years — he enrolled at

George Washington University to indulge in his life-long passion for poetry and he learnt to play guitar — but perhaps this message on The Walkmen's website forum says it best: "I went to college with Stewart Lupton in New York, and lived down the hall from him. He used to sit in the laundry room at 4am typing on this ancient typewriter. He was a real presence no matter what he was wearing, or doing. I figured he'd probably become fantastically famous, and drop dead of a heroin overdose before 30. Fortunately, the latter never happened. Sadly, neither did the former."

THE STOOL PIGEON: Hello Stewart.

STEWART LUPTON: Hey, how are you? Good morning... um, what time is it there?

SP: Quarter past six in the evening.

SL: Happy sunset!

SP: Where are you?

SL: I'm in a pick-up truck with my friend Carole, my lady friend, and we're going to spring her 17-year-old badass son from a shitty boarding school in upstate New York. A very covert mission. And I'm gonna stop by New York and see the band, hang out for a bit, maybe go to a museum or something. We're gonna stay in one of these hotels that have been erected in the last five years in the neighbourhood where my old band used to live in the early nineties before Giuliani cleaned it all up [the Lower East Side]. They overlook the tenements where there used to be chicken fights on the roof and eight drug dealers per block. They're nice hotels but I feel like I'm betraying my roots or something [laughs]. There used to be nothing around there other than fortune telling ladies with no customers. Now there are Asian fusion restaurants and little waterfalls and stuff like that.

SP: Looking forward to seeing the band?

SL: Sure.

SP: There has been a line-up change since the mini album was recorded.

SL: In a sense. The mini album was basically me — I did it with a drummer [Hugh McIntosh] and this girl [Betsy Wright], and everything else I did myself, other than Judah [Bauer] doing a little guitar work. The drummer is pursuing... I don't know what you get after a PhD. Put it this way: he's 27 and he's never not been in school. I think he's got, like, nine letters after his name. The girl has unfortunately dropped off the grid.

SP: Introduce your new band for us.

SL: New band? I forget their names. I'm kidding. Paul Boring [Arfield] plays guitar, and he's formally of a group called The Stiffs. You'd like them — they're Anglophiles. Their whole thing is The Addicts, a little bit of Buzzcocks, and a lot of Wire, Sherlock Holmes and old turn-of-the-century surgical instruments. My old band did our first round-the-country tour with them. Fond memories. The bass player, his name is Tunde Oyewole. He's a Nigerian chess master and a lawyer on the side. It gets in the way. He needs to scale that back a little bit. Tunde has played with me, on and off, for about five years. There was a period when I was just playing acoustic guitar and he played stand-up bass behind me. And then our drummer now is one of the best drummers I've played with in a long, long while. His name is John Melville. He used to be in a band called New York Loose. I don't remember them but they had a foxy blonde girl singing with them.

SP: It seems you've intentionally left a lot of space in the Childballads music, at least compared to Jonathan Fire*Eater. I think you called it 'roomy' and 'warm'.

SL: Exactly. If you don't really have finality, then you can't be judged [laughs]. We got this review from *The Guardian* after we played a show at the Metro bar in London — our first show as the new band, the guy forgot to mention — saying that they were basically like a bar band. I thought that was great. I don't think they were that happy about it, but there are all these fucking bands on MySpace clambering to have their own identity, like The Horrors or The Hives or whatever, and I like it that my band is kind of anonymous. It's just chords — Paul doesn't play a single lick. He has another band called Beaut and with them, because they're only two people in the band, he does all these amazing loops and effects. The time is coming when we're gonna start weaving some of that into what we do but, so far, it's just been chords — an anti-style. By the end of the European tour there was definitely some personality leaking out, but right now we're just concerned with trying to be a band, getting the changes right and feeling good on stage. It's nice not having a girl in the band and dealing with three guys [laughs].

SP: The second show you played was supporting Cat Power at The Forum, also in London, the day after. How was that?

SL: Fantastic. We played really early but it was at least half full. I got really emotional because playing in 2,500 capacity theatres was kind of where I left off 10 years ago. We were almost at that stage. And, to be honest, that's my life's goal — my life's dream is to get to that level again. I don't want to get any higher — I don't care about MTV or any of that stuff — but to be able to fill beautiful theatres that size, metaphorically and literally, would be very satisfying. The most comfortable I felt on the whole tour was playing there. I arrived early, walked around on the lip of the stage and I loved it. There's a formality and respect about theatres like that. You go to these fucking little dingy-ass nightclubs and what's the aesthetic? Black? There's something about theatres and town halls that's handed down. You really have to hone your mind to think about it and realise what it means, because it means a lot.

SP: You've been playing a Bob Dylan song in your set, 'Walls Of Red Wing'. Has he been a big influence on your new music?

SL: I guess so, but I play it down now because the fucking Walkmen have all of a sudden become Dylan-esque. I've been obsessed for a long, long time, but I'm trying to get over my obsession and be a bit more, er... I'm not a record freak anymore. I don't know.

SP: So you feel a sense of rivalry with The Walkmen?

SL: I used to say there wasn't a rivalry with The Walkmen, but I got back to New York feeling elated with my new bandmates and our success on the tour — it was a really surreal thing because I hadn't been to Europe for eight or nine years and I finally made it back behind British microphones off my own steam — and there were fucking Walkmen posters everywhere, and fucking huge ones, too. You know how they do those posters on buildings that cover windows up and they pay the tenants? I always wanted that because I thought it would be a great way to make rent... Anyway, they had these posters up in New York for the Flaming Lips and the Yeah Yeah Yeahs and The Walkmen. They did a tour promoting Camel cigarettes too — eight-date tour on the east coast — and they got 20 grand a show. Fucking ridiculous. These are the same people that had this pseudo-Fugazi, five-dollar X on the hand, church basement righteousness and turned down Calvin Klein, which I wanted to do and frankly I think is a little bit cooler than doing a song for the *Spider-Man 3* soundtrack. So the answer to your question is, 'Yes, I'm ready for a full-on rivalry with The Walkmen.' They're really starting to piss me off. Can you print that in capitals?

SP: Sure. STEWART LUPTON IS READY FOR A FULL-ON RIVALRY WITH THE WALKMEN BECAUSE THEY'RE REALLY STARTING TO PISS HIM OFF. But aren't you just jealous?

SL: I'm jealous of the money and nothing else. I could do what they're doing in my sleep. I already did that. I respect their work ethic but their music interests me about as much as the New Jersey Turnpike. It's as bland as the New Jersey Turnpike. I actually liked the *Bows & Arrows* record but I really don't think the whole Walkman thing is any good anymore. I feel great! I've never said anything like this before. You're gonna get an exclusive [laughs].

SP: Do you ever see them?

SL: We're cordial, but there's tension and there always will be. I'm jealous of the money. I'm a writer and a poet and there's not a lot of money there. And I'm jealous of the fact that they have a fucking manager, and a van. In fact, they probably have a bus. But I've already passed them artistically with this new EP so I don't sweat too much at all. It's not hubris, it's just objective empirical reality. The first thing I did after Jonathan Fire*Eater broke up was this country acoustic thing with Judah — it wasn't country, more, I don't know, folk — because I was really into the five-CD Dylan *Basement Tapes* box set and some other folky records. I was so fed up with the screeching fucking doorbell organ we had in Jonathan Fire*Eater and the preciousness of it all. It was so impersonal. I'm happy with the way things are now. Artistically, I sleep fine.

SP: You were relieved when the band broke up? I thought it upset you deeply.

SL: I was fucking destitute. The thing I did with Judah was eight or nine months later. The band breaking up was the final blow: my house of cards came down and the world gave me an *ass-whooping* that became one in a series — the anthology of kicking the shit out of Stewart Lupton started then, then it reached volume eight, and it's abated for the moment, but there's still some tension between me and the world. So, yeah, I was torn up. We were best friends and I was an only child. I met Walt when I was seven or eight years old — the second day after I moved to Washington DC from South Carolina. We were inseparable. What we talked about doing when we were 15, we did. How could I not have been upset?

SP: It seems when the band did get together and moved to New York, you were super ambitious. You knew you were good and you wanted fame. Is that right?

SL: Hell yeah! But there's a difference between ambitious and preciousness and hubris. And there's false humility, arrogance,

101

narcissism and knowing whether you're good, and we knew we were good. Where's the bar? Was it other bands? No. We never thought about ourselves in relation to other bands, just whether we could make the hairs on the back of the neck stand up. We'd stumbled upon this sound and it was like splitting the atom for us — a big discovery. I remember the series of practices — the two or three when we uncovered our identity, sonically. It was exciting, but, you know, er, that's a novel...

SP: Do you still feel the same ambition?

SL: Definitely. I admire that about The Walkmen, too, but they don't have it anymore. It's a slow burn and they should just quit. They don't have the artistic ambition — some of them are married and they have babies and they want the money. Their quality of problem is more like whether they should buy a beach house or whatever and I'm sweating for what I can find. I lost a penny loafer in Paris and had to get on a plane... but that's a lot better than it was. Seeing The Walkmen on David Letterman on a tiny little TV in a very, very bad state with, you know, debris all over my room... it's been difficult. I actually have a Walkmen t-shirt in my bag and I do like those guys — I'm just trying to sound tough and it feels good.

SP: Really break this down for us, Stewart. Is Childballads a proper comeback? Are you truly serious about getting out there again?

SL: It will probably fall apart in about three months, I bet. Why not? Either that or it will stay together and it'll happen. If it stays together, the dominos will fall in a really interesting place and I'd be really excited for that. It's 50/50 — it may just implode, or we might pick up a pattern. People expect that of me — to get my shit together for six months and then fuck it up. It makes record executives sheathe their Montblancs [laughs]. I'd like their pens to come out with a little more ease from their breast pockets. But I'm in it for the long haul. I don't know what will happen. I feel good and my ambition is bigger than it's been since Jonathan Fire*Eater. For everything — for poetry, for writing, and girls, and girlfriends,... that's the bulk of it, but I could be a... what do you say over there? Tosser? Wanker? Prat? I could be a prat and point to some bands and stuff and ask for some royalties or something... I guess I feel like rock'n'roll owes me like a back cheque, but I'm not pretentious about it — I really don't think I contributed that much. It just sucks to be this poor. It's ridiculous. I work hard and... I don't want to get into it. It's the horse. The cart is filled with money, but the horse is a war horse.

SP: Are you nonetheless proud of the huge influence you and Jonathan Fire*Eater had on the generation of New York bands that came after you? I'm thinking particularly of The Strokes, Yeah Yeah Yeahs, Interpol...

SL: If they pay me my money, I'll say, 'Yeah.' The Strokes owe me! I'm fucking around, but it is becoming apparent to me. There's a woman making a documentary about all that and she started off with me, and now I think she's making it only on me. But I don't have any bitterness, it's just rock'n'roll.

SP: You can't say you don't have any bitterness! You do sound bitter.

SL: I was just taking the piss, as you say. What are you gonna do? Get an attitude about someone wearing the same clothes as I used to? Or parting their hair like I did? I wouldn't be functional if I thought on those terms. But it is fun to fuck around with it. Everything I've said about The Walkmen, it's like playing ping-pong. These things don't govern my life. The money part does a bit, and that sometimes makes me think of other things because these bands like The Strokes and the Yeah Yeah Yeahs, they're millionaires. The Walkmen probably are, too. Millionaires! I don't understand that — it just doesn't compute.

SP: When Jonathan Fire*Eater signed with DreamWorks, that was a million dollar deal, wasn't it?

SL: Yeah, but that got so fucking manipulated by the press. It was for a three-album deal that we didn't complete and do you know how much we had to give to the lawyer? And to the agent? And we got our manager's whole mouth re-constructed because he had no teeth. Eight hundred dollars a month — that was what I got paid. Less than the minimum wage. And we got $10,000 each upfront. That was fun, but it was gone very quickly. The whole thing with that deal was totally blown out of proportion. And please don't think I'm bitter — I'm not, it's just that sometimes the bare facts are depressing.

SP: So you don't feel like you're owed something?

SL: No, not at all. I'm fucking around. If anything, I owe life. A lot. I've extracted a lot of life force from the natural flow of things and manipulated it for my own pleasure, and then set about planning and constructing my own downfall. I've been gone. No one owes me shit. I don't look for handouts. At all. But the bare facts are that my best friends are millionaires. Maybe you don't understand. We slept on the floor of the van... I don't know. And maybe they're not millionaires, but they're very well-heeled and, I don't know, it's just bizarre to me more than anything else. I don't have any resentment, or any sense of entitlement — it's just bizarre and I'll admit that it does sting a little bit. That's it, and then I move on. And here I am. Wait, we're about to go through a tunnel. I hope I don't lose you.

SP: Still there?

SL: Yup, I can hear you. Let me read you what it says on the back of this truck that's in front of us: "If convicted murderers get life, why do innocent babies get executed? Think about it. Choose life."

SP: That's pretty heavy.

SL: That's America, man. [pauses] Yeah, so I would like to start a full-on, blood-thirsty, going-for-the-jugular thing with The Walkmen. Just for fun.

SP: What have you been doing all this time The Walkmen have been putting records out? There was stuff online saying you were dead.

SL: When I read that, I was like, 'Okay, time to start something.' I've been studying. I'm a writer, I went back to college and studied poetry. And I fell in love with a woman and lived with her for five years, almost got married. I lived life, man. I cleaned up my act, fell again, got back up, dusted myself off. It's the work of life. I was writing the whole time, taught myself guitar... There was a point when DreamWorks were going to fund me as a solo artist. They gave me money and I got this most precious guitar, and I got to meet Robbie Robertson from The Band. He was working as an A&R at DreamWorks. So depressing. He was never one of my heroes but, you know, he breathed the same air that Dylan did. First thing I asked him was, 'What's the name of your tailor?' He hated that. Then I asked him how Richard [Manuel] was, because I forgot he killed himself in the eighties. My feet were way down in my mouth, but he was a prick and I don't give a fuck about his Native American electronica bullshit. The Band sucked. They were great when they had Bob Dylan, but name a good record they ever did by themselves? So, what was I doing? All that stuff. And not paying attention to contemporary music. It's kind of a drag keeping up and knowing what bands sound like what. There's just so much shit. And then I'm told I have to be associated with MySpace and that's a lot of pride to swallow. Everyone has to be associated with MySpace! Where did that come from? It's so Orwellian. It's like having a fucking microchip in your brain. It could get worse and it will get worse.

SP: What music have you been into recently?

SL: I still love Royal Trux. For me, they were the well to go to and they still are. They're so misunderstood. No one will understand for 100 years how good they were.

SP: A lot of people have been saying there's a bit of Royal Trux about Childballads...

SL: They're definitely an influence, but I'm trying not to copy them. I'd like to borrow more of their spirit and their bravery and their tenderness and their sincerity, though.

SP: Mind if I ask you about drugs?

SL: Are you gonna take something? What do you need?

SP: When you were away doing your own thing, everyone assumed you were stuck in some kind of heroin-induced hell. Is heroin something you're still battling with?

SL: Is heroin something I'm still battling with? [pauses] Um, life is something I've had to battle with and, I don't know, poppies are a part of that and... yeah, it's no joke.

SP: So you haven't left it behind?

SL: I haven't what?

SP: Left it behind.

SL: It's in the rear-view mirror — it's back there but I've got a pretty healthy distance from it. But I don't take it for granted. It could be round the next corner or whatever. But it's not looking like it.

SP: Did it suppress your creativity?

SL: Did it suppress my creativity? It suppressed my respiration. I don't know. I don't know. I think that, er... I mean, what do you call creativity? I suffered. Really. [pauses] I'm not gonna get into this. I went through an extremely disproportionate amount of suffering at a very young age, and I saw and did things and got into the wrong car and went into the wrong bars. Every place I went was the wrong place at the wrong time. I just got beatings — psychic beatings, over and over. So, when you come out of that, you've got something in your gut that ain't ever gonna go away and that's where my courage comes from.

SP: Do you find it hard to trust people now?

SL: No, man. The reverse. That's where my love comes from — I trust people. Even if they're lying straight to my face, I trust their good nature or whatever.

SP: Do people find you difficult to trust?

SL: Sure, yeah.

SP: No more than any other person?

SL: I would say probably more. Addiction does things to your thought process and your points of relativity. Basically, it's like all bets are off. You're in a matrix. It's not real and it seems like it doesn't matter if you have to tell a little white lie, or six or seven, or 100. I was suffering a lot and I'm a much better person now. And a lot of it is directly because of it.

SP: You're 32 now, right?

SL: Yeah. You know about Saturn Return? I talk about it so much, I've got it down and it's very like what we've been talking about in the past minute or so. In your late twenties Saturn returns and basically anything in your character that's not nailed down, or any lids that are not closed, or if you've got any unfinished monkey business... all that shit gets thrown back in your face and strength grows exponentially. When you emerge from that, that's when you're ready to start playing again.

SP: Have you emerged?

SL: Oh, hell yeah. It's all in the rear-view mirror.

SP: Tell us about Francis J. Child, who you named your new band after?

SL: He was some pretentious hack who recorded 300-and-something ballads and he said [adopts pompous voice], 'There are exactly 376 songs, no more, no less, and I've collected all of them!' He was an appropriator but he had some style. Our name has nothing to do with him — a little bit but not much. But I love his songs.

SP: Is the cover of the Childballads record based on the Elizabeth Bishop book of poems, *Edgar Allan Poe & The Juke-Box*?

SL: It is. And I think it looks good. I love Elizabeth Bishop — she's one of my patron saints.

SP: Isn't she a bit like Emily Dickinson in that she didn't get much recognition until after she died?

SL: She smokes Emily Dickinson! Eats Emily Dickinson for breakfast. Poetry and rock'n'roll are like stock — your stock comes up, your stock goes down.

SP: Got a literary tip to end with?

SL: Ever read that T. S. Eliot poem 'Gerontion'? It's the one that starts, 'Here I am, an old man in a dry month / Being read to by a boy, waiting for rain.' It's an old man reflecting on his life and inaction — the Hamlet thing — what he's done, what he hasn't done, and what he's left undone. There's this one section... I can't read it without getting really worked up. He says history is too much too soon, and too much in too weaker hands. The timing was wrong. We had the right prayer but we were praying to the wrong god. You could apply it to so many things. It's trying to do something but you keep missing. Everybody tries and everybody just gets fucked. Everybody tries and everybody falls. Basically it says that your motives are pure when you're young and then they go south and decay. Then you're left with a character that is not able to fit—a round peg for a square hole. You have most of the ingredients but not them all.

INSIDE THE GATE

An email to S____, about a day spent with Jaz from Killing Joke.

By Tony Gunnarsson
From issue 4, Autumn 2005

Oh man, interviewed the singer from Killing Joke on Thursday. That was fucking crazy. P____ told me the band were in a studio recording vocals for their new record and I should go down, and of course I was over the moon thinking that I'd be able to hang out with old timers and maybe hear some new songs. Alrighty! I get the address (off Pitfield Street in Hoxton), turn up and find out the place is essentially a squat. A white stoner dude with dreads opens up and I walk in to find three old geezers smoking the puff-puff-jammy and drinking rum and cokes. The singer, Jaz, who looks a bit like Andy McCoy from Hanoi Rocks (black long hair, cowboy hat), starts chatting a bit and then everything suddenly turns into some sort of ex-criminal, ex-junky and white-Rasta convention. The talk is about dealing heroin back in the eighties and some other shit. After a few drinks and some I-hope-no-one-is-noticing-that-I-am-not-actually-smoking-but-making-it-look-like-I-am business, I'm pretty much part of the gang. He he.

Then the door knocks and in walks this fucking douchebag called David Sinclair who's *The Times'* pop critic. He's there to interview them for some CD biography or whatever. The professional journalist (notice the contrast with me — by this stage I'm starting to feel at home, glass of rum in hand, and so much the amateur journalist that I haven't even turned on my dictaphone or even mentioned the interview I'm supposed to be doing) looks like one of the Rolling Stones (same generation) and definitely has some sort of public school background. He's dressed up in a vintage-style denim jacket, *à la* Hawkwind in 1968, that he probably bought at Rokit (Brick Lane branch) for £185, and an Indian-style shirt with some fancy stuff on it. "Oh, the sixties were so hot, man," his clothes say. He acts like he's at Buckingham Palace.

After a little while, the geezers, minus Jaz, retire to the basement to listen to the mixes (luckily, the music coming from down below was loud enough for me to get a sneak preview, but more about that later) and the pro, the am, and the rock star sit down at a table. Dictaphones and papers are brought forth, and the journos prepare their assault. The rock star pours a fresh round of vintage Jamaican rums, served ice-cold with coke (although the pro journo declines, which reminds me of how the police are in the comic books I read as I kid — "No thanks, I never drink on duty") and battle begins. Questions are fired left, right and centre, and Jaz responds in broadslides of proclama-tions and monologues lasting as long as 30 minutes. Hashish smoke, broken glasses, snus, Killing Joke CD-Rs, half cigarettes, wax candles and a copy of *Decline of the West* litter the battlefield and produce a magnificent panorama of human consternation. The discussion is 90 per cent made up of Jaz's constant but intelligent delivery on subjects like global warming ("There will be a noticeable difference from March next year... air-flight will be the privilege of the rich"), his influences, literature, art, booze, drugs, etc.

After 1.5 hours, the pro from *The Times* declares his intention to leave. "I will certainly have this day to remember, Jaz," he says. I stay on to talk with Jaz on a more informal level. The engineer, whatever his name is, suggests a Vietnamese on "K" (meaning Kingsland Road — old slang?), and we all head out to eat, drink more and talk about further interesting subjects — Easter Island, Israel, women, Iceland, tours, records... Finally, I say my goodbyes and stumble home. Job done.

Killing Joke are playing soon, dude, and I can't stress how much we need to go — not only because their singer gave me free booze, or because I am totally unable to write anything sensible about them after enjoying such surprising hospitality, but because the band, which I have naturally been listening to every day for the last few weeks (not to mention a whole lot in the past), are something weirdly unique. I am unable to define why, but I guess it comes down to their first record from 1979, which is really great. And now, after 25 years, they're releasing another record, which is just as good as their first. (Oh, I shoulda said that they've made records all through those 25 years, though not all good.)

In a few words: they are poetic in their message and they're more than just another band — not because they've been at it for 25 years, but because they genuinely work hard. They rehearse every day (what other dinosaur rock band do that?) and Jaz says things that he means, like: "If we can't make a contribution to innovation, we may as well pack it in."

Damn, I am starting to sound like a freak now. Let me try another angle...

Here's a very short line from their song 'Seeing Red', which is on their last album: "They are dropping bombs again / And they're doing it in your name." I like it because of its simplicity. It's fucking CLEAR. The governments are killing in our names. AGAIN!

Overall, though, Killing Joke are seen as being something of a doomsday band — you know, singing about 'the end' and nuclear war. But they have been largely misunderstood. What they are saying is: "The end is near, but don't worry — life goes on and we should celebrate it in the meantime." I find this extremely attractive. It is anything but the "let things just be" attitude that seems to be common nowadays. Theirs is a message of rationale, intelligence, aesthetics AND life. Don't ignore things, they're saying, but make sure you — and this is a very important aspect of Killing Joke if I understand them correctly — DANCE LIKE A MOTHERFUCKER!

Get it?

Let's go to this show, get drunk and dance.

Here's a quote from Jaz that tells you something about them: "We were really cynical about the music industry. We saw groups that had high ideals and then, when they had come out through the machinery, they'd lost all of their ideals. We did not want to end up like that. So, our first question was: 'What do we want to achieve out of this?' And the answer was: 'We wanna inspire other people to do whatever their gift from God is.' Or whatever their 'true will' is, as we call it. So it was a renaissance at the end of the day — to inspire other people. We had this idea that Killing Joke is a mirror. And what you see in us, you can do, too; that the stage is an audience and the audience is a stage."

Thanks for listening.

DANCE THE DABKE

Twenty weddings a month, 500 albums, influenced by no one.
Omar Souleyman: number 1 in Syria.

By Kev Kharas
From issue 22, Summer 2009

The four men onstage are playing their hit. It doesn't sound like any hit I've ever heard before — a kind of jacking Arab trance music with a pulse twice as fast as the one in your arm, tinny, blaring and squabbled over by boa-goading solos, flanged absurd and played, alternately, upon what sounds like a battered Casio keyboard and some kind of electronic lute. Stage lights switch right and expose the other pair: one, a pot-bellied poet, whispering improvised peels of verse into the left ear of the man they're here to see, crowd rapt at his skull-to-ankle djellaba robe, his seventies bad cop aviators and the unwavering bristles of his thick, black moustache. He strides forth from the poet, barking metre aloud and it echoes back so that each of Omar Souleyman's words banishes the next like street clamour competing for city air, those frantic solos still weaving in and out of the mix, the crowd half-maddened now, 'Leh Jani' hustling on.

Omar Souleyman claims he's the most famous pop star in Syria. "Number 1," he says through an interpreter, holding his index finger up and out towards me to make the point clear, a smile forming beneath the 'tache and the glasses he's worn since injuring his eye aged six. Joined by his nose, the three most dominant features of Omar's face form the outline of a pair of weighing scales. I stopped listening to what he was saying a while ago — the interpreter, however valiant her efforts, can only distil every 50, 60 words that Omar and his collaborators say down into two or three, so for large parts of the interview I give up on nuance and questions about the politics of 'world music', just nod when it seems right and gaze at those scales, weighing up Omar's righteousness. The most famous man in Syria is sat in the back room of the Boston Arms, a hovel preserved by the desperate, daytime Irish drunk. I'm dubious. Again, I weigh him up. Fame must work differently in Syria.

"We started on a local level, among the people. Our music started as a hobby, with traditional folklore. I began singing when I was seven — people told me I had a beautiful voice," he says, dodging further questions about his past and what he would be doing now if it weren't for the music, jumping from the age of seven to the start of a career that "got serious in 1994", when he started playing wedding parties.

"My family didn't like it at first — they didn't think it was a good thing for me to take up and they forbade me from playing the parties, but I kept doing them and started getting famous. Everyone knew my name and people were always asking for Omar Souleyman. That's when we realised we could do it and after that my family were okay with it, and, thank God, in the last two years it's all been positive."

Now Omar, who's 41, and his small gaggle play over 20 of those wedding parties every month. So far, only 20 of their releases have been studio recordings — the other 480 or so were all made live at some point in the last 15 years, duplicated onto tapes and distributed to the cassette kiosks across Syria that seeded Omar's fame. The harsh, electronic tones arranged by composer and synth virtuoso Rizan Sa'id jar against the precious sounds of the Syrian classical tradition, and because of that Omar's music enjoys a slow-grown folk infamy that would be impossible to achieve in the UK, simply because things don't stay invisible for that long here (the only recent example that springs to mind is donk, interestingly, though I doubt there's much demand for Blackout Crew CD packs in downtown Damascus). 'Leh Jani' may have won Omar Souleyman TV coverage and hundreds of thousands of YouTube hits of late, but there's something undeniably and irredeemably street about his troupe's hysterically overdriven racket, dismissed by his home nation's cultural cognoscenti, according to a recent *Wire* feature, as "music for taxi drivers"; as "nothing".

Omar's is a mongrel, villager music. He, like Rizan and regular poet Mahmoud Harbi (who chain-smokes onstage and is kept from this European tour by family problems) was born in northeastern Syria, far from its capital and closer to the borders of Turkey and Iraq. In a sense, you could see their uniqueness derived as much from isolation as it is from being surrounded.

"We're famous in all pockets of the Arab world," Omar says, "and our music is a mixture of Iraqi, Kurdish, Turkish and Assyrian because the village we live in borders all those different nations nearby..."

"We haven't been influenced by anyone," fires back Omar when the question comes up. "There's no big hero for us and we don't listen to other music. We don't copy anyone. We wanted to use all those influences so people would like us, but also because no one else has done it before."

The music that Omar's group play — their "jacking Arab trance music" — is a newly electrified take on a traditional style known as 'Dabke', which is also the word given to its accompanying dance, a jig sped up by Sa'id's Korg synths that herds rows of men and women into line, sometimes sexes separate, sometimes together, but always holding hands, their bodies bound in a unison jerk.

The use of raver electronics to extend, rather than sabotage, the Syrian musical tradition is what sets the outfit apart from both high-minded traditionalists and the Westernised pop they hold in so much scorn. The equipment also harbours practical advantages, the keyboard's built-in sampler allowing three people rather than six to make the trek from village to village for the next wedding party.

"Once someone tried to play a trick on Omar," Rizan says. "They gave us the address of a party 200km away and asked us to play. When we arrived, we knocked on the door and the guy standing there was completely confused. 'There's no party here,' he said. We were annoyed, but people started to hear that Omar Souleyman was in the village and we went out and there was a whole crowd waiting for us. They all heard Omar was there because people had been talking — they all recognised his style, his look."

I turn my gaze back towards Omar, who's sat flanked by Rizan and Mahmoud's sub for this tour — that pot-bellied poet Zuhir Maksi. He leans back and nods sedately, his aviators reflecting everything back out towards the room and once again my eyes hang awkwardly between the lenses and the moustache, unable to detect recognition in either. I ask about copycats.

"People hear all the music we put out and they listen to how it's played. 'What are they doing? What are they doing?'" says Zuhir, the poet turning mimic.

"They listen to what the words are about and then they copy it," interjects Omar. "Sometimes they take our songs, sing the same words, dress up like me, make a video and then they play it on television and there's nothing we can do about it because we don't have copyright laws in Syria."

Isn't that flattering in a way, I ask him?

"Yes," he says, grinning again. "It makes me more famous."

Go, now, to YouTube, and search for 'Omar Souleyman TV Clip' and behold the trappings of Omar's fame. Dancing girls! Lecherous, sword-flaunting sheikhs! A man dragging a pair of obstinate goats, presumably intended for imminent slaughter! My dubiousness vanishes as eyes burst at the rainbow of gaudy Arabic titles, advertising logos and a number — 095627233 — that frame the clip. I wonder who's manning the phones at the other end of those digits? In the midst of it all is aviatored, unflappable Omar, the calm in the mirage.

"My stance on the stage is different from other musicians," Omar explained to fellow Pigeon Luke Turner recently.

"I don't like to move, I don't dance and I don't go down off the stage. During a wedding, the people make a circle, holding hands. I stand in the middle, but I don't dance. My words and the music make people dance."

There's not much hand-holding a couple of days later when Omar makes his London debut, but there is movement — dancing — which is rare enough for shows in the capital. Rizan, Omar, Zuhir and the fourth along for this European jaunt — a beaming, bullet-fingered bazouk player called Ali Shaker — are joined onstage by two Arab men with video cameras and a loose medley of people who I recognise from the interview as associates of Sublime Frequencies. The label specialises in going beyond the trite representations of world music drip-fed into western consciousness to track down the sound of distant streets, but rarely could their efforts have been greeted so warmly. The two men onstage put down their cameras and take each other by the hand, jerking their bodies to cheers from those amassed, getting sweaty at the pits.

I remember what the interpreter told me two days previous about how "surprised and shocked" Omar and his gang have been by the response thus far from this foreign continent and "how they've met with an audience that they love and that loves them, even though they don't understand the words".

What are the words about?

"They speak of love, and sadness, and happiness," comes the staggered response from behind glass lenses.

"They're probably the same as English words, but the music is different."

More raucous. Less sappy.

"Yes. That's just our way over there and the way we work here is the way we work at our weddings at home."

I size him up one last time, this squat, stony-faced, Syrian wedding singer hidden behind his weighing scales.

Can you dance the dabke, Omar?

"I can dance the dabke," the interpreter interprets.

Omar smiles. Do I doubt him? Would I dare?

THE CUNTOID IS A LEMMINGHEAD

Or, a not so fruitful encounter with a re-born grunge band and its hostile leader, Evan Dando.

By Ash Dosanjh
From issue 9, December 2006

Don't get me wrong, I entered into this interview with Evan Dando sincerely wanting to like him; to talk through his latest album, *The Lemonheads*; to tweeze out the odd anecdote or two about his drug highs and lows; to filter through his stormy relationships with grunge starlets; to explore his music collaborations; and just plain old get to know what sort of guy he really is. But what we want and what we get are two very different things.

For those that don't know, The Lemonheads have gone through some sort of a renaissance this year, reforming after a considerable hiatus and releasing a whole new long-player. But the fact that most live reviews of their recent UK tour have cited Karl Alvarez and Bill Stevenson of seminal punk band Descendents as making up the current line-up is pretty indicting — of the state of current music criticism, and of the opinion held of The Lemonheads in general.

Actually, Devon Ashley and Vess Ruhtenberg from The Pieces have been filling in on drumming and bass duties. But what does that matter when The Lemonheads' recent 'reformation' is just another expansion of the Evan Dando franchise. Since he formed the group with high school friends Ben Deily and Jesse Peretz, he's changed the line-up almost as often as Mark E. Smith has with The Fall. Both are egotists that know what they like and who they don't (not necessarily a bad thing, considering the choice music they've produced with their bands), but there is a difference: Smith pretty much stands by what he says and has probably never apologised to a journalist. It's a testament to his sense of conviction. Dando, on the other hand, has constantly proved himself to be both thoroughly disagreeable in interview situations

118

(again, no bad thing — if he wishes to get stoned and not talk, that's his prerogative) and something of a flake. Or cunt. I've not decided yet, and I'm not alone in railing against Dando. In the past there have been fanzines dedicated to hating him (Jeff Fox's *Die, Evan Dando, Die!* being a case in point), and at Glastonbury '95 he was booed for turning up hours late for his set.

My acrimonious meeting with the one-time luminary of nineties grunge after a gig at Bristol Academy was followed up the next day with a call from his PR proclaiming how "worried" Mr Dando was about our encounter. I bet he was. But I guess this had less to do with his obnoxious behaviour towards someone who'd travelled nearly 200 miles to meet him and more to do with the fact the ageing rock star had let his tongue wag rather frivolously. And about all the wrong subjects, too. Naughty Evan.

It turned out that Dando wanted to have another chat — to set a few things straight. But before we get to that, let's have a look at the exchange of words between Dando, Ashley, Ruhtenberg, Dando's wife Elizabeth Moses (for a model, her face is pretty fucking greasy), some strange snotty girl called Kath (who blagged her way backstage because she'd met Evan at Glastonbury some time ago, aged 11, when her dad was a doctor there), my friend Tom and me. If it sounds absurd, it's because it was.

The interview was supposed to take place earlier in the day. But when push came to shove, Dando and Co. were nowhere to be seen. Phone enquiries from tour manager Hugo revealed that Evan was still at his hotel. The Novotel in Bristol. "He was supposed to be at the venue two hours ago," Hugo told me. Apparently he couldn't find a taxi. Having lived in Bristol for three years, I know that every other bastard car on the road is a cab. And according to the AA's route finder, the hotel is exactly 1.1 miles away. You can walk it in less than 20 minutes.

I was told the interview would take place after the show. Fine. So I watched Dando on stage safe in the knowledge that I'd been guaranteed a meet. He seemed in good spirits. Banter was limited, but the smile on his face was evident. Songs old and new were churned out pleasantly enough and sing-alongs among the crowd were frequent. His temperament boded well for our interview. Or so I thought.

Evan Dando: "Hey, sorry for earlier. I couldn't find a cab."

Stool Pigeon: "That's cool."

ED: "Hey, do we have to do this now? Can we do a phoner or something?"

SP: "Well, I've come a long way for this interview…"

ED: "Okay, but make it quick."

Alarm bells start ringing. Dando seems more interested in playing with his wife's iPod than talking. But Ashley and Ruhtenberg were more than accommodating — charming, even.

SP: "What's it like having the band together?"

ED: "It's great. It's really fun. It's like, er, we're gonna be on the road from December 17, so you know something's gonna happen, you know? It's really fun. I went down to Indiana and we practised for a week."

Devon Ashley: "We practised straight for two weeks. It was like boot camp or something. Rock'n'roll boot camp."

SP: "Was it like being a teenager again?"

ED: "Yeah, definitely. Who has a cigarette? Okay, let's finish this interview. Put the timer on. Put the timer on!"

SP: "How long have you been in the UK?"

ED: "We've had a good time."

SP: "I asked how long."

ED: "Three weeks."

SP: "Where are you based now?"

ED [looking at Vess Ruhtenberg]: "Oh, you're interviewing me and I'm just being a total pain in the ass by trying to bring in the rest of the band into the whole thing."

SP: "I'd like to know about the others, but I asked you first."

ED: "I dunno, you guys just write what you want. I dunno how to help you. I really don't. I'm tired."

SP: "Are you happy with the new album?"

ED: "Not particularly, actually."

SP: "Why?"

Dando doesn't answer the question and instead goes off on an unsolicited, lengthy and boring rant about his record label. At the end of his monologue I say, "You sound bitter," to which he replies, "Okay, it's done. The interview's done."

"Do you really object to doing an interview?"

"Not at all. It's just the timing was off. That's all."

And that was all. Despite Dando waking up the next morning deeply concerned about what he may or may not have said about the hands that feed him, emails batted back and forth to his PR over the course of a week trying to sort out a follow-up interview revealed that he'd done a Lord Lucan. Pity. I would have enjoyed telling him he was an utterly vile and spineless moron (fancy getting someone else to try and cover up your mistakes), but I'd also have liked to mention that he's really made a comeback album to be proud of (even if the better songs were written by Bill Stevenson and Tom Morgan).

P.S. Dear Evan, I feel sorry for you, because you're a fool, and have only neglected to mention certain aspects of our rather drab conversation out of some lingering respect for your achievements. For any future interviews you intend to carry out, might I suggest that you ensure your wife keeps her trap shut, even when she thinks the dictaphone isn't on. Ta ra.

FISH'N'CHIPS GUY

Tricky Comes Home

By GARRY MULHOLLAND
From issue 17, Summer 2008

They used to call him Tricky Kid. They still could. The 40-year-old Tricky still looks ridiculously fit and ridiculously young in his black, skinny-fit t-shirt and khaki combats. His hair is a mass of dreadlocks, piled on top of his head. He is enthusiastic and extremely talkative, as if he's been bottling up conversation since 2003, and is just desperate to communicate.

We are at the west London offices of Tricky's new record label, Domino, also home to Arctic Monkeys, Franz Ferdinand and The Kills. He's kicking off the promotion for his first album since 2003, *Knowle West Boy*, and he's already done one interview with me on the phone from his current home in Los Angeles.

Knowle West Boy is his best album since 1998's *Angels With Dirty Faces*, and his most accessible since his much-loved 1995 debut, *Maxinquaye*. It's his most varied and frivolous record, with a range of different (and previously unknown) co-vocalists, a cover of Kylie's 'Slow', and self-confessed tributes to favourites like Tom Waits ('Puppy Toy') and his beloved Specials ('Council Estate').

Knowle West is the area of Bristol where he grew up as plain old Adrian Thaws, and the album is a deliberate attempt to re-connect with his roots as well as his English audience after living in America since 2001. The likes of 'Council Estate' and 'School Gates' are acutely autobiographical, and contrast neatly with the likes of 'Cross To Bear', which is inspired by Martin Scorsese's *The Last Temptation Of Christ*. It's the first Tricky album which could legitimately be described as fun.

Both on the phone and in person, he answers every question revealingly, without pausing to think about how he might be perceived.

The only time that he betrays interview technique is when I compare him to fellow nineties Bristol scene graduates Massive Attack and Portishead: he very quickly and cleverly distances himself completely from what they do.

Some of his quotes, in the cold light of print, sound like hip hop braggadocio — about girls, money, his work. But they don't come off that way in person. His description of his working process is the most unpretentious and self-deprecating of any musician I've spoken to, and his staccato West Country accent takes much of the edge off of his more declamatory statements.

He says a lot of funny things, but never laughs at his own jokes. His energy and honesty are disarming — the polar opposite of the moody, paranoid hardcase that the media presented him as in the late-nineties. He immediately makes you feel like his mate, and that you're having a chat in the pub, although, very occasionally, his attention wanders, as if there's something important he should be doing. "I'm a very fish'n'chips sort of guy," he insists. "It's easy once you meet me to see there's no difference between us." And this is sort of true, except for the unconscious eccentricity that often separates geniuses from the rest of us. For example, on the one hand, he has total recall of events from 20 or more years ago. On the other, he's so flaky with the present that two of the *Knowle West Boy* songs — 'Veronika' and 'Joseph' — are named after the vocalists, because he's lost their details and doesn't know how else to track them down. He couldn't do the same with the female vocalist on 'Bacative' — she's the sister of a friend of a friend who was passing by the studio. Tricky doesn't even know her given name.

The two lengthy interviews give me a lot of material about the new album. You sense that first single 'Council Estate' means more to him than anything he's done before, partly because of the autobiographical lyrics, but mainly because it pays musical tribute to The Specials, and it's The Specials that first made him "dream I was in a band", as he puts it. He also talks at length about the film that he's directed to promote Brown Punk, the label he co-owns with legendary ex-Island owner Chris Blackwell, which he hopes will be in cinemas next year.

But space is limited, and I decided to sacrifice a lot of the stuff about his latest projects in favour of the hilarious, poignant, occasionally angry and occasionally scary anecdotes about his past. It's these stories that give you a real insight into why Adrian Thaws grew up to be such a maverick, and why so many journalists have found him difficult. It's all very well wetting yourself over corporate American gangstas, but when the real British working class thing is sitting in front of you, middle class boys are inclined to be intimidated and more than a little disturbed by the less glamorous realities of a genuinely tough upbringing.

THE STOOL PIGEON: The early signs suggest that *Knowle West Boy* is attracting more attention than any album you've made for a long time. Are you relieved?

TRICKY: I'm satisfied with it, so I don't really give a fuck what anybody else thinks — fans or music people. I think it's a good album. After five years... it ain't a comeback album. I've been doing stuff. But it is five years and I really wanted to make my presence in England known again. The fact that people are interested in me is a bit of a relief, in a way. But I'm still quite naïve about the business. If I only had two interviews to do, I'd still believe there was interest. My ego, you know?

SP: You moved to New York in 2001. When we spoke before you admitted that England had made you jaded.

TR: Yeah, jaded. My life had become a cycle of album and tour. And I was tired of people looking at me. Tired of people asking me stuff... a guy in the street just now asked me if I was in *The Fifth Element*. Tired of that shit. I missed the times like when I was a kid growing up in Knowle West, and I was just one of the crowd. There's a lot less pressure on you. It starts making you paranoid, walking into a club and everyone's staring at you. I come from a place where you didn't wanna be seen. We used to steal cars and break into stores and put on leather jackets and do runners. Coming from that to everybody

124

recognising you... I get real paranoid if someone looks at me — I think they want a problem with me. So you're always on guard. Always on guard.

SP: So you went to stay with family in the Bronx...

TR: I was living in New Jersey, I had a cousin in the Bronx. That's where I chose to hang out. We hung out with this reggae soundsystem. One of the guys is Rod — or Rodigan — who is the reggae singer on 'Bacative' and 'Baligaga' on this album. They had a house with a wall knocked down in-between and a studio, and people used to just come in and chat. We used to hang out outside this Jamaican restaurant. And I had a few friends in Manhattan and it was just clubs, bars, parties. I had three or four girlfriends — a girl in New Jersey, two girlfriends in Manhattan, and a girlfriend in Connecticut. And it was just like... chaos. But the main thing was that, apart from the core people I was with, no one knew who I was. I was just a kid hanging out on the street. So no one would really give a fuck. There were 30 of us going to a club and no one would notice me. Just smoking weed and drinking.

SP: You weren't making music at this point?

TR: No. Then I went to LA to make music for [blockbuster Hollywood producer] Jerry Bruckheimer. He's such a good guy. He set me up in a studio in Brentwood. I'd go there every day, make five real dark tracks, and five more commercial tracks. And every time, guaranteed, he'd choose the darkest. I thought he'd be quite different. And I got kinda stuck in LA because of 9/11. Then I made *Vulnerable* in 2003. And then I didn't do anything — not recording, not writing lyrics — for about three years.

SP: What made you start again? Was it difficult getting back into it?

TR: I got to a point where... I've got a kid who's in school. It costs a lot of money. All of a sudden it's like, you'd better start working! I'd been living off my money and just partying.

SP: Have you done well enough out of music to just take three years off, then?

TR: Yeah. But I was doing crazy things. I used to have a car service what cost me 200 grand a year in New York. From New Jersey, it would take me to a club, I'd come out of the club at six o'clock in the morning, the car service would take me home, I'd sleep for a few hours, shower, get back in the car service and do it all over again. I had a house in New Jersey, two apartments in Manhattan, and a hotel room for partying. Buying an ounce of weed a week. So I've done very well out of music. I bought one of my cousins a £16,000 bracelet, sent my kid to a good school, bought Martina [Topley Bird, his former musical partner and mother of Tricky's daughter] a house which she rents out. But it still reached a point where I'd better start working.

SP: So was it hard motivating yourself to work again?

TR: Nah! Because I still love being in the studio. When I sit around, I tend to think too much. When you're in the studio, you don't think about your problems, so it wasn't hard at all. And my fanbase deserved another album from me. I owed people. But it took me a long time to find the right label. I had some really terrible meetings. Executives saying things like, 'This is a hit song if you have a middle-eight!' You just pick up the CD and walk out. A year went by. Epitaph [the US indie founded by Bad Religion guitarist Brett Gurewitz on which Tricky made two albums and also signed Tom Waits to its sub-label] was a great label but they never had no presence in England. This is my home country. I'm moving back at the end of this year. So Domino seemed perfect.

SP: How do you go about composing? Do you play many instruments?

TR: Keyboards. But I don't really play. I'm still very naïve. I don't really know about music — I'm a one-finger guy. I remember I was in Japan once, and all the press wanted to come into the studio, and I'd never done that. They were watching me make this track and were all

126

waiting for something magical to happen. And at the end, one of the Japanese guys comes up and goes: 'Ah! Golden finger!'

SP: Listening to 'Council Estate' on the new album made me wonder what it was like for an unusual black boy growing up in what you've described as 'a white ghetto'. I mean, you like wearing women's clothes, for example. Did you get a lot of hassle from the kids around you?

TR: No, 'cos I've always been weird. So my friends didn't expect any different. The first time I wore a dress was at 15, out to a club in Bristol. I wasn't the toughest guy among my boys, but I was the leader. I was always with loads of people, but by myself. I had no inhibitions. I think that was a lot to do with my grandmother as well. She never forced me to go to school. She let me go to clubs at 14. I come from a criminal background, so the first thing she'd say to me is, 'Take anything out of your pockets that can ID you.' 'Cos I'd be out robbin', and most people get caught by leaving a school report behind, or something. She taught me criminology! I remember Martina saying to me once, 'You've got no discipline.' In my family, getting caught was bad, but going to jail wasn't bad. So you think that was normal. Putting on a dress... I didn't give a fuck what people thought. That comes directly from my family.

SP: Where did the name Tricky come from?

TR: Krust! Do you know Krust? [Yes: Bristol drum'n'bass veteran and member of Roni Size/Reprazent.] There's a place called Broadwalk Shopping Centre, and when I was about 15, I was supposed to meet him there. But my uncle from Manchester had come down and I got in the car and drove straight back to Manchester with him. About six weeks later, I come back. My uncle dropped me off at Broadwalk... and Krust was there. It was like he'd been waiting there for six weeks! So he says, 'You tricky bastard!' And that was it... I got the name.

SP: The whole Wild Bunch-derived Bristol scene of the late eighties/early nineties — Massive Attack, Nellee Hooper, Smith &

Mighty, Roni Size and Krust, Portishead — did it feel like you were in the centre of a creative hotbed?

TR: Nah. Because not everybody… Smith & Mighty and Wild Bunch were the biggest things. I remember Rob from Smith & Mighty wanted me to do a track with him, but 3D [Massive Attack's Robert Del Naja] was against it. Everybody was very separatist. So it didn't seem like there was a movement. It wasn't competitive, but it was cliquey. Also, they didn't want Knowle Westers in certain clubs. I saw a different kind of racism. I saw my friends being beaten up by the police and they're white guys, and I'm a black guy but I haven't been touched. It was a class thing. So I always felt like a bit of an outcast. Knowle Westers were stigmatised. We weren't wanted anywhere. When I joined Wild Bunch, the likes of Daddy G [Massive Attack's Grant Marshall] and 3D couldn't go to Knowle West… they would've got robbed.

SP: You spent time in jail, is that right?

TR: Hmmm. For forgery of the Crown. I had all these forged £50 notes and had all these kids going round to stores. I did one myself, stupidly. My uncle got murdered, and at the funeral I went into a store. Plain clothes turned up, punched me in the stomach and cuffed me up. One of my friends grassed me up and I had to go to Horfield Prison. But only for a few months. I was in youth custody, so I must have been 18 or 19. When I first got back to Knowle West, it was like a coming of age… I felt good. But I didn't have a good time in there. It wasn't the violence or whatever. It was little things. Like the food. And talking to someone and asking, 'How long have you got?' and them saying, 'Three years,' like it was three minutes. What scared me was that you could get used to this – the food, the boredom. It wasn't for me. I never went back.

SP: When you were getting bad press in the late nineties, do you think it was because the largely middle-class journos just didn't understand someone from your background?

TR: In a way, yeah. A mixed-race guy who people saw as black, talking about Kate Bush and crossing-over. People didn't know how to handle that. And people were putting everything down to race. There were misunderstandings and a bit of fear. People still have a perception of me as a moody, dark dude. The press made me look hardcore. It takes a while for people to warm to me because of that. But the press have done great things by me too, so I can't complain.

SP: There were incidents at the time that made you look bad. Weren't they true?

TR: I was somewhat to blame. I don't regret anything, and I was responsible. But I'm also bright enough to know that they were responsible as well. Like the guy from *The Face* magazine [Craig McLean, who was assaulted by an associate of Tricky's in the late nineties]. This was outrageous! He came to Atlanta to interview me... I don't even remember his name anymore, but the guy did not like me. He started to fuck with me. He asked me things like, 'Why do you hold Martina back?' And I told him the truth, which was that when we first signed to Island, me and Martina were going to be called Maxine Quaye. Island were very against that 'cos I was already known as Tricky. That's why it was my name. So the press wanted to talk to me. I tried to fob press off on Martina, but they wanted to interview me. So there's your answer. Then he started on, 'She's a one-parent family. You've basically abandoned her.' I *still* pay for my kid to go to school. Me and Martina talk every day. I just didn't like the way he treated me. So... I see him at Glastonbury. He starts arguing with me. He's drunk as fuck. He called me an animal. Now, I had people with me — people from my family who don't know about this music industry. They didn't understand it. So one of my family knocked him out! Then in the press it's like, 'Tricky knocks out editor of *The Face*!' But if you're fucking with the bull, you're gonna get the horns. I was standing behind my uncle waving at the kid, going, 'Don't!' So I couldn't do anything right after that.

SP: But, ironically, *Maxinquaye* was labelled a 'dinner party' or 'coffee table' album...

TR: It was weird to me. Not so much the coffee table thing, but...
it was seen as intellectual. I'm far from being intellectual! I thought I'd
be a ghetto artist.

SP: But the music you made and make sounds nothing like R&B
or 'urban' music...

TR: Yeah. But I saw what I made as totally natural. I listened to
The Specials, I listened to Public Enemy... Really, I had a different
upbringing with music. The first time I heard Bob Marley was from a
white kid in Knowle West. When I was growing up I would stay with
my cousin and Miles Johnson from The Wild Bunch. And while they
were getting ready to go clubbing — and I was too young to go out —
one minute they'd be playing David Bowie, then it was Funkadelic, then
it was Marc Bolan. My music background was very diverse, and I took
it for granted that everybody's was like that. If I like Kate Bush,
everybody does. Realistically, people from where I come from don't
know who the fuck Kate Bush is. It's all an accident.

SP: When you started working with Massive Attack, were you
aware that this was The Big Break?

TR: No. It went from fun to... not so much fun. When we got a
record deal and my friend Miles left the band, the music changed.
Suddenly people were worrying about what you said on the mic. I
wanted to do some Jamaican cursing on one track and 3D wouldn't let
me. To be honest with you, when Massive Attack signed a deal I was
getting £200 a week and a pager, which meant I didn't have to go out
and thief. It was just work. After a while, I didn't turn up in the studio.
They did a video once called 'Where's Tricky?' I was hanging out with
my old friends and still getting into a little bit of trouble, even though
I'd done prison. But to me, Massive Attack were a hustle. I wasn't
interested in being famous or being a star. It was just... survival. I didn't
like the manager, Cameron McVey. I didn't understand what he was
about and I don't think he liked me from the first time he seen me.
Coming from my background, I was still suspicious of everybody. It

was Miles Johnson and Claude Williams who got me in the band and they left... Mushroom's the only person I hang out with now and again. They weren't really my mates. When I was in a court case for two years in Oxford, not one of them came. Not one of them visited me in jail.

SP: It does seem like everyone from Massive Attack's early days has fallen out with them one-by-one...

TR: It's 3D. The only guy left in Massive Attack now is 3D. He's always wanted to be a pop star and The Wild Bunch weren't like that. Shara Nelson wrote some of them songs and it would have been good for them to keep doing singles with her. But 3D got threatened, thinking she's gonna take over the band. She got fucked over. Mushroom [Andy Vowels] got pushed out. 3D's very ambitious. He's a control freak. He wants to be a superstar. I ain't got no beef with 3D 'cos I left of my own accord. But I could totally see what was happenin'. As soon as Shara blew up on that single, he was threatened by that. She was still on wages. That's why he's the only one left. Why would he get rid of Mushroom and Daddy G? [Daddy G has rejoined Del Naja for the new Massive Attack album, to be fair.] Originally, 3D was brought in by Miles. He was a kid that used to hang out with them and try to get in the band. He loved The Wild Bunch and used to do graffiti and stuff. All of a sudden he was in the band. And then his ambition took over the band. So really he's left on his own. But I don't know if that can be a great life. He had all his mates around him making music, and now he's by himself. Pretty depressing, in a way.

SP: 'School Gates', on the new album, is about you making a girl pregnant in your teens. Is it about Martina?

TR: No, it's about a girl called Malika. She's half-Jamaican and half-Spanish. Basically, I met her when I was a kid, about 15. And at that age I wasn't really into girls — I was into money. I was always looking for somewhere to rob. But my mate liked her mate and asked me to get off with her while he got off with this other girl. Next thing, I'm with this girl. We were going out with each other for years and I used to wait for her outside her school. She got pregnant when we were 16 or 17. She said to me that the kid was mine, but told everybody else that the kid wasn't. I've only seen the kid once, when she was three, and she looked exactly like my daughter, funnily enough. Some people still think she's my kid. And I don't really know how to handle that. Do I just turn up? Does the kid know I'm supposed to be her father? I'd like to find out, but it's kinda hard. This is something I've really got to sort out. I don't wanna just turn up in this 23-year-old girl's life and say, 'I'm supposed to be your dad.' I need to go and see her mum, when I have some time to go to Bristol.

SP: Blimey, I don't know what to say. Let's go onto another song from the new album, 'Puppy Toy'. It's a duet with Leeds chanteuse Alex Laws, and if you just take the lyrics *you* sing, it's a typical 'all women are gold diggers' hip hop theme. Except that you give the woman in question a very funny and aggressive right-of-reply all the way through the song.

TR: Yeah. I was brought up by women. A lot of the men in my family were in jail. I was disciplined by a woman. I grew up watching the women in my family having street fights. I've seen my grandmother fight men outside grocery stores. My uncle Martin did 30 years in jail, on and off. My auntie Maureen, she got remarried, and this guy was not from the world we were from. And my uncle kept going round smashing up their house, drunk. So one time, Maureen came out, threw pepper in his eyes, and stabbed him in the stomach. Twice. So women, to me, are just as gangster as the men. A lot of my lyrics are written from a woman's point of view, like 'Broken Homes'. That's why I need female vocalists. I wish I could sing like Janis Joplin or PJ Harvey. But I can't. The female singer on 'Past Mistake' and 'School Gates' is my ex-girlfriend who I've just had a horrific break-up with three months ago. And it's funny, we wrote 'Past Mistake' when we were good, but it had started going bad. Her name's Lubna Mhaer. She's a French-Moroccan from Nice. One day we were in bed listening to it and I'm like, 'Wow! This is about us!' It's like I knew this was gonna... I hurt the girl, know what I mean? Sometimes I write songs and it's only later I know what they meant. There were a few songs on *Blowback* that could've been talking about 9/11, but were made before it. But with 'Past Mistake'... I didn't really love her properly. I loved her like a sister, not a girlfriend. And I was willing to stay with her because she's family. But we kept arguing and arguing. Even though I weren't in love with her, I changed for her. I wouldn't fuck around with other girls. I was thinking of having kids with her and marrying her. I was happy. But for some reason, she wouldn't give me a breather. She won't speak to me now. So 'Past Mistake' is about me and her.

SP: Who's the male vocalist on the haunting 'Joseph'?

TR: He's a busker! He's a young kid, around 22, just trying to earn money to stay in LA. I met him outside a food shop and he just played me something, right there and then. And Queen Latifah was sat there! It was very weird. I said to him, 'Call me tonight. Here's my number.' And Queen Latifah was like, 'Wow! You're different.' 'Cos apparently you don't give your number to buskers. She is the coolest lady... I've got to know Latifah since then and she's a beautiful person. Anyway, he came round, I gave him lyrics and a melody to sing, and he did it. I've called the song 'Joseph' 'cos I'm hoping he'll hear it and get in touch. 'Cos I've lost him and I want to work with him again.

SP: Fidget house don Switch co-produced a couple of tracks on your album, including 'Council Estate'. What's he like to work with?

TR: He's a good guy. But he'd listen to these tracks with live drums and say, 'Do you want me to change these to electronic sounds?' And I'd say, 'Why would I want that?' People have a perception of me that I'm the Electronic Kid or something. But I wanted live sounds. He does things like M.I.A., which ain't really my thing, to be honest. She's a talented girl but I've never been into all this trip hop shit about new music. I don't know if there is any new music and I ain't trying to chase anything, or be part of any scene. I'm not a dance artist. So then he started to understand what I was sayin'.

He probably didn't think I was right, but that's his world — the clubs. And I don't give a shit if they play my music in clubs. He was like, 'But your fanbase...' and I was like, 'I don't care about my fanbase. If I make an album I like, my fanbase'll like it.' I was once talking to this hip hop guy, suggesting things he could try. He said, 'Nah, my fanbase won't like it.' I said, 'Well, get another fanbase then!' You can't be dictated to by your audience.

SP: So what *do* you listen to?

TR: Hip hop. Earlier today I was listening to Capone-n-Noreaga. Public Enemy and Rakim. I still listen to The Specials and Kate Bush a lot. Some of the Britney Spears new album. Fucking wicked! A band called Paleface — a very underground band from Nevada. It's like white NWA. Not a lot of new stuff, to be honest with you. There's a girl called Hope who's done a wicked track — you can only find it on YouTube — it's like a traditional love song... beautiful. I like some Arctics stuff. I still listen to The Stone Temple Pilots. And Nirvana.

SP: You, Portishead and Massive Attack have all made 'comebacks' this year. Suddenly, nineties Bristol music is on everyone's radar again. The Portishead comeback was an unexpected commercial and critical triumph. But still people refer to what you all do as 'trip hop', a term all of you hated...

TR: Well, that doesn't bother me because I'm so different to Massive Attack or Portishead. And my fans seem to realise it. I haven't heard the Portishead — it's not a band I listen to. I don't listen to Massive Attack. So I'm in a totally different world.

SP: Is it true that Portishead's Geoff Barrow engineered your very first single?

TR: No, he was the tea-maker!

SP: Do you wake up sometimes and wonder how a teenage criminal from Knowle West managed to become a globe-trotting pop star?

134

TR: Yeah! Especially as my grandmother's 85 now and she's never even been on a plane! I've always felt like I shouldn't be here but somehow I got my foot in the door. It's a bit of a piss-take, in a way. Like it's all some surreal movie. Sometimes I feel like I don't deserve it. That's why I needed to take time out after *Vulnerable*. I'd started to take it for granted. I needed to be taken down a peg or two.

RUDE AWAKENING

Forced party vibes, terrorist porn, and a return to pop for a band in which hope springs eternal, Sonic Youth.

By Luke Turner

From issue 22, Summer 2009

Late April and Sonic Youth have just finished their first rehearsal for *Later... with Jools Holland*, unaware that tradition dictates they'll have to join Depeche Mode, Lily Allen, blues legend Taj Mahal and US soul singer Raphael Saadiq in a boogie woogie jam to open tonight's prerecording of the show.

"Are you serious?" asks Kim Gordon from behind her big dark shades.

"It's a forced weird-party-vibe thing," Mark Ibold informs her, and he knows: his alma mater Pavement were forced to play along with Jools Holland and Co. back in the 1990s.

Sonic Youth were on *Later...*'s first series, before the opening trial by piano and portly gent in jacket had been invented. Then, a slimmer Jools called them a "rude sound" before they played 'Sugar Kane'.

"I don't remember doing it last time we were on," says Thurston Moore with a disbelieving tone. "We were on, like, the sixth episode. It has to be boogie woogie? I'll boogie woogie with him."

There was no boogie woogie at the Scala in King's Cross the night before, nor the interminable jamming that often marks/mars Sonic Youth gigs. Playing their most intimate UK gig in years, the band ripped through new album *The Eternal* and a greatest hits set to a rabid reception. "Sonic Youth are the best thing in the entire fucking world!" screamed one fan. Others gazed upon the racks of guitars on either side of the stage in awe. It's sometimes hard to understand the level of devotion that Sonic Youth engender. They might be loud as hell and unimpeachably hip, but all too often there's something curiously detached and overly self-aware in their music. At their worst, they fall for the most unfortunate kind of pompous self-indulgence, be that Kim Gordon walking in muddy boots along her bass at Glastonbury in 1998, or the onanistic doodling of last year's retrogressive *Daydream Nation* Don't Look Back concerts.

The Scala gig, though, couldn't have been further removed from these two extremes. Like much of *The Eternal*, the set was punchy and abrasive, and it was telling that Sonic Youth played three tracks — 'Brother James', 'Making The Nature Scene' and 'She Is Not Alone' — from their earliest days in New York. Inspired by the brittle sounds of no wave on one hand and Glenn Branca's guitar experimentation on the other, Sonic Youth were formed by Thurston Moore, Lee Ranaldo and Kim Gordon in 1981 (current drummer Steve Shelley joined in 1985), releasing their first record, the 'Sonic Youth' EP, on Branca's Neutral Records in 1982. Largely ignored in their homeland, Sonic Youth began to pick up support in Britain and Europe, with Paul Smith's Blast First releasing their second album *Bad Moon Rising* in 1985 and continuing to distribute subsequent LPs in the UK until the band signed to the major Geffen Records to release *Goo* in 1990. A marked departure from the psychedelic noise of its predecessors, *Goo* was arguably Sonic Youth's first out-and-out pop record, and it was followed in 1992 by *Dirty*, which upped the commercial ante and followed a tour alongside Nirvana.

After *Dirty* and its follow-up, *Experimental Jet Set, Trash & No Star*, Sonic Youth retreated from the upbeat post punk-influenced sounds that brought them their greatest success. Still on Geffen, they began to release a series of largely instrumental pieces on their own SYR imprint alongside their studio albums. Jim O'Rourke joined the core quartet for the release of *Murray Street* (2002) and *Sonic Nurse* (2004), only to depart and be replaced by Ibold in 2006. *Rather Ripped*, released that year, was Sonic Youth's last album for Geffen before they signed to Matador and returned to the shorter tracks and poppier dynamics that characterise *The Eternal*.

It's perhaps wrong to read too much into the band's decision to return to the independent fold. *The Eternal* material had its genesis long before the band signed to Matador and Sonic Youth have never shied from trying to infiltrate the mainstream by any means possible. Indeed, from album artwork to lyrical subject matter and song titles, they've attempted to subvert the iconography of America, of rock'n'roll and pop culture, bringing together high and low via the medium of feedback and peculiarly tuned guitars. Whatever the case may be, the Scala performance was that of a band full of vigour and vim and clearly relishing the opportunity to demolish such a small venue. Afterwards, Thurston Moore lolloped around the aftershow like an overgrown teenager, and Lee Ranaldo chatted to Nick Zinner before being taken off to meet renegade Special Jerry Dammers.

If only their enthusiasm extended to the interview the next day.

Tuesday morning, 11am. Sonic Youth have finished their first *Later...* rehearsal and want to go to Shepherd's Bush's gleaming new Westfield shopping centre. Steve Shelley, however, opts to stay behind in the BBC dressing room, which resembles a hotel that was last expensive in the 1970s.

"Steve doesn't go to malls with journalists," says Lee Ranaldo. "He doesn't like them to see the kind of store he goes to. That's what it is. The kind of store he gravitates towards is not very rock'n'roll. I can't tell you where he goes, though, and Mark... Mark's the one for cookware."

"Since he joined the band, he's always been decked out in gothware," quips Thurston Moore, about Sonic Youth's newest member. "He likes to shop in Hot Topic."

Thurston Moore heads towards Foyles in search of a couple of books, though he's trying to curtail his hoarding habit. "I did used to collect books, but I'm trying not to collect anything any more. Reasons of space, and I think it's offensive given the state of the economy," he explains. "I want to get rid of a lot of stuff. I've always been into collecting records and books and other ephemera. I want to do a real purge but it's hard, unless you get a collector to come and rock away with everything. I could set up an eBay store, but then I'd have to stop touring."

Kim Gordon, who is 56 today, doesn't seem to want to be doing an interview. She's already made it known that, because there's no make-up or stylist on hand, she's not going to have her photo taken. Apparently yesterday's press day was a bit wearing. "We're kinda sick of photos," she tells *The Stool Pigeon*'s snapper, Dave. In her blue jeans and effortlessly expensive-looking black leather jacket, she strides off towards Top Shop, a favoured UK stop-off for the full-time musician and part-time fashion designer.

Lee Ranaldo, on the other hand, wants to go to HMV to hunt out some DVDs. Gliding up a silver escalator, the check-shirted guitarist spots a mall staple. "We did a record with Starfucks... er, Starbucks," he says. "It's interesting because it was kind of a compilation — celebrities picking their favourite Sonic Youth songs. When we put it together we thought it was going to be the biggest sell-out of our career. At the time we did it, Starbucks was the only company in America that had figured out how to sell records when all the labels were falling on the floor. But by the time ours came out... it's the rarest record we've ever released. It's impossible to find in the shops. I don't know how many they made — literally a few hundred."

Ranaldo is looking for a particular Japanese animation DVD. "It's ostensibly for my kids," he says. "Someone told me it was out in Britain and not anywhere else. It's the new Hayao Miyazaki — his last movie — I can't remember what it's called. I wanted to get the new Dylan album, but that'll be cheaper at home. Oh, they're playing the Dylan."

He spots chic terrorist flick *The Baader Meinhof Complex*. "There's another terrorist porn film that we were into recently. It's called *Eight Miles High* [2007 German film, *Das Wilde Leben*]. It's about a German commune where this beautiful girl becomes a real famous model. She became the face of this German commune — a free love commune."

His shopping habits reveal typical Sonic Youth schtick, the sort of thing that's influenced and been explored in their work from their earliest days until now: ultra-violence, cults and mass murder translated into a stylish, well-executed aesthetic.

"I don't go to the mall back home," says Ranaldo, waiting for an

AWOL Moore and Gordon, "but we should have had the four of us in some terrible mall setting. We can do photos of the men of Sonic Youth in the women's lingerie section of that store."

But Kim Gordon, it appears, is still not keen to have her photograph taken, and the chance to snap the men of Sonic Youth in pantyhose is spoiled by over-zealous security guards.

The lanky guitarist and singer returns with a copy of *Michael X: A Life In Black And White* and a very obscure looking novel with a sleek, minimalist cover. His plans for an end to hipster hoarding have clearly gone awry, and he tucks the books under his arm as he walks down the wide new road back to Television Centre.

"I can sort of see a relationship between some of *The Eternal* and *Dirty* in terms of the dynamic," he says when asked if the new record is a nod back to Sonic Youth's more pop-orientated moments. "We definitely wanted to make songs as opposed to doing an avant-garde opus. That was one idea we had, now that we're on Matador: to do just one unending composition — something really radical. But we decided that they're a really strong song-supportive label, so we hadn't practised doing that to such a degree last time around."

"It was interesting that we'd just done the *Daydream Nation* shows — revisiting these songs that the four of us had done together in our early trajectory," Ranaldo interjects. "Some of those songs had an energy that we'd kind of forgotten about, and some of that energy and the experience of doing those songs impacted on the new record. We've been really into what we're doing over the past few records, but it hasn't been that full-on or in-your-face, balls-to-the-wall thing. We swing from record to record and, like Thurston said, the next record might be one long 20-minute piece on each side. It just kind of goes back and forth — we don't plan too much."

Was it good doing something new after the *Daydream Nation* gigs?

"What's cool is we've gone through this period with Jim O'Rourke where we were this real solid quintet, then we came down to a quartet, which we hadn't been for almost 10 years and did *Rather Ripped*," Ranaldo explains. "Immediately after that we revisited *Daydream...* as a quintet, and those two points were pretty instructive. We were happy with *Rather Ripped*, but we were also pleased with what we were doing with *Daydream*... It's like a snapshot of ourselves over three different periods."

Back in the BBC studio, it's time for Sonic Youth to run through their rehearsal to camera. A runner sits peeling labels off of bottles of Becks, and replacing them with *Later*... branded stickers. Except he's got the wrong series, and has to do it all over again. The bottles of beer are empty. Onstage, Sonic Youth are a machine. Guitars are picked up, they plug in and, bang, 'Teenage Riot' blasts across the studio. Serious-looking operators in black combat trousers swing camera booms or scurry around the studio floor at the behest of a bolshy looking lady wielding a clipboard. Lily Allen appears in scruffy jeans, gives a thumbs up and sits, nodding along. It might be part of the routine — a gig for technicians and a few people sat around the back of the room — but Sonic Youth look as if they're enjoying themselves up there. "Earth to guitar player," jokes Moore when Ranaldo makes a mistake. When the rehearsal's done, said guitar player makes sure he takes time to thank the floor manager before Sonic Youth hop across in front of Lily Allen and back to their dressing room.

There's some furtive whispering and urgent discussion between Ranaldo and the band's manager. Sonic Youth and entourage gather in the hallway and it transpires that, finally, Kim Gordon has deigned to join the rest of her band in a quick photoshoot. Everyone troupes outside to the hallowed courtyard of BBC Television Centre to be snapped in front of T. B. Huxley-Jones's statue of Helios, Greek god of the sun. The west London sun has disappeared behind ominous-looking grey clouds and a light drizzle falls as, a roll of film exposed, Sonic Youth clamber into limos. Mark Ibold is off to the Sir John Soane's Museum and Seven Stars pub. Thurston Moore, ever the big kid, wants to go to a fancy hotel for a cream tea. "Clotted cream, scone, English tea and tequila slammers," he cries.

A few hours later and Sonic Youth are back in the studio that crackles with the tension of live telly. Jools Holland calls for a riff from Raphael

Saadiq's guitarist to start the boogie woogie jam. Thurston Moore humps the amplifier with his guitar. Lee Ranaldo attacks his with a drumstick. Kim Gordon, in a short skirt that few women her age would dare to wear, batters massive rumbles from her bass. From the other side of the studio, the noise is at atonal odds with the session muso wibbling from the other groups. Sonic Youth clearly still know how to make the "rude sound" in the hallowed court of Jools.

When the show is aired a few days later, the camera pans around the room: Raphael Saadiq, Taj Mahal, Depeche Mode, Lily Allen, now in a little black dress. Sonic Youth's exertions towards a rambunctious disruptive intent are visible but, curiously, none of the sound they're making can be heard through the television speakers.

SLEAZE & CARACAS

Venezuelan salsa, ska, socialismo, getting drugged and robbed, and why El Comandante Hugo Chávez doesn't mind people burning CDs he likes.

By Ben Jacob

From issue 22, Summer 2009

Barbiturates and *burundanga* nearly killed me. It began in the low-lit, pulsing crowd of a salsa club. Sheet music and pictures of baseball heroes covered the walls. Seven old men played on congas and cowbells, timbales, trombones and double bass. One crooned into a silver mic. Their music whipped shadows into whirling knots of arms and smiles, glistening flesh, flashing eyes. They probably didn't know they were playing what could have been my funeral march, and those dancers didn't know they were in the presence of a soon-to-be-almost corpse. Even if they had, they may not have cared. Two things are cheap here: petrol costs about $1 to fill a car and a contract for a killing is $200. This is Caracas, a divided city, and capital of Venezuela, a country that stretches from palm-fringed Caribbean beaches, to the steamy Amazon, from the snow-capped Andes, to the *Llanos* grasslands. For over 150 years, Caracas has been famous as the birthplace of Simón Bolívar, leader of South America's revolution against the Spanish Empire. Nowadays, an estimated four million people call this tangled nest of motorways and skyscrapers home. It has the second biggest barrio on the continent and is infamous for the highest per-capita gunshot death rate in the world. Some say 30 people are killed here a day; some say 50.

Three days after I was drugged, after doctors expressed surprise at my survival, after drips, scans and hallucinatory insects scuttling around my peripheral vision, I passed the city morgue. At 50 metres, there was an overpowering stink. It drowned the city's ambient smell of fried food, rubbish and fumes. Pedestrians clamped tissues over their mouths, but it struck me as a sweet perfume. I had been unconscious for 17 hours, yet my kidneys had not been harvested. I had not been kidnapped. I was not yet a victim of this city; not yet one of its dead. The smell of those decaying bodies was, for me, the smell of life and, because I survived, let me describe the soundtrack to this city; the angry fog of horns and grunting engines; the bells of ice-cream sellers; pneumatic drills; street hawkers; car alarms; wailing sirens; squawking parrots and buzzing insects. Venezuelans detest silence, and an inescapable and integral part of this soundtrack is music.

Salsa dominates the airwaves. More than music and dance, it's a cultural necessity. Every boy's mother tells him, "If you don't salsa, you'll never get a girl." Live salsa bands play to crowded clubs most nights of the week, but it's not all salsa: international, national and local groups of all genres find airtime in the capital. Music is piped into metro stations, blared from buses and taxis, shops, bars and cars. When this music is Venezuelan, it is often a mixture — a blend — like the drugs which I was fed. The traditions of Colombia, Cuba, Puerto Rico, the Caribbean, North America and Europe combine with more typically Venezuelan sounds, which are, in themselves, diverse. The descendants of African slaves still dance to the beat of *tambores* in the streets, whereas popular folk music — the *joropo* and Venezuelan *gaita* — finds its heritage in the grasslands. Just as Venezuela has geographical variety, so its people are from different cultural backgrounds, each bringing their own influence to a unique fusion of instruments, rhythms and, more recently, politics.

"*Gaita*." Ruben shakes his head. "You hear it most around Christmas time, but the songs are nothing about wise men and angels. They sing about whatever they want. Traditionally they sing against the government, the system — it's been that way for years. They are an exception. In the eighties and nineties here, there was much more music against the system — like punk in Europe, making people think about where and how they are living. Now in Venezuela, protest bands are very underground. Even some *gaita* groups are banned. It's part of the crisis we're having. The government controls the media and the radio. It won't let protest bands be heard. It tries to stop people speaking out against The Process."

Ruben Perez, ex-DJ, now voice-over artist and one of my guides through the Caracas music scene, is driving me to a gig by Babylon Motorhome, one of the city's most interesting collectives of artists and musicians. It's night-time. He drives one-handed. With the other, and without paying much attention to the road, he sorts through the CDs that lie like silvery leaves spread around his car. He selects one, slips it into the dashboard. It begins to play: Los Amigos Invisibles (Invisible Friends), an internationally popular Venezuelan six-piece combining Latin rhythms, disco and acid jazz. The music jars with the view through the windscreen: street corners buried under rubbish, walls daubed with graffiti portraits — of the President, Che Guevara, Fidel Castro — and pro-socialism, pro-Chávez, pro-The Process slogans, which Ruben dislikes.

In simple terms, this Process is the Bolivarian Revolution, an 'anti-imperialist', 'democratic-socialist' movement spearheaded by the country's charismatic President, Hugo Chávez, who was first elected to power in 1998. Named after Simón Bolívar, over the past decade, the Bolivarian Revolution has brought great changes — from the slightly bizarre (changing the country's time zone and its name, from Venezuela to The Bolivarian Republic of Venezuela) to wholescale social reforms. Among these has been the distribution of vast petro profits from the country's oilfields to the underprivileged majority. This mostly occurs through policies called Bolivarian Missions. Among other things, the Missions import Cuban doctors to provide free healthcare and mobile clinics, which drive into the traditionally no-go barrios; free access to education; improved housing, sanitation and subsidised food. The intention is to encourage deprived people to gain a sense of self-worth and, ultimately, the means to provide for themselves.

Needless to say, for the poor, who had been repeatedly ignored or exploited for decades, these changes have led to a real sense of national inclusion and pride as well as immense appreciation for the President. His supporters, *Chavistas*, can indulge their devotion to El Comandante by attending rallies and receiving free gifts of Chávez calendars, badges, t-shirts, posters, flags, hats, and even Chávez dolls and action figures.

This may sound quite alien to an outsider, but Chávez's allure and his policies' humane touch is such that others — not just the underprivileged — have also turned towards it to support the Bolivarian Revolution's ethos of equality, opportunity and South American unity. On the other hand, the rich, like Ruben, insist on seeing a more sinister side.

"They say, 'We are not dictators — you don't see tanks in the streets,'" he mutters about the Chávez 'regime', "but you don't need to see tanks to know what is happening."

Opponents to Chávez criticise the fact that, to benefit from some of the social projects available, people must join his PSUV (United Socialist Party of Venezuela). Others accuse him of seeking dictatorial power; they condemn spiralling crime rates and inflation, increasing restrictions on personal and national finances (since 2003 Venezuela has been a closed economy and its own currency — the Bolivar fuerte — is worthless abroad); controls on the media, and growing investment in military projects.

Despite these grumblings, for now at least, El Comandante seems unstoppable. A few times a week, national TV channels broadcast his live, hours-long monologues; his face is plastered across billboards and posters, graffitied onto walls, and appears in murals beneath slogans like 'Patria, Socialismo o Muerte' ('Motherland, Socialism or Death').

In this mix of hope, politics and propaganda, music has assumed a role in spreading the revolutionary message.

The Nuevo Circo de Caracas is an early 20th century construction, which makes it ancient in this city plagued by redevelopment. Situated in a neglected sector of Caracas, aside from the gaudy yellow and red towers of the entrance, from the outside, it looks like a circular concrete motorway overpass. Inside, it's more like a low-key colosseum with rings of seats descending to an oval arena. Until 1997, toreadors fought bulls here. Nowadays, the Circo is dwarfed by skyscrapers and hillsides covered in the mottled brick of San Agustín barrio. The arena is currently occupied (with the tacit support of the government) by one of Caracas's artist collectives. The tunnels beneath the stands that once echoed with the cries of crowds and dying bulls are home to free yoga and drama classes. Free concerts are sometimes staged in the bullring. Today, a green-haired girl on a unicycle practises on a terrace once reserved for VIPs, vultures wheel across the blue sky and a man sitting beneath the stands listens to salsa on a radio. The tune's an old hit by Oscar D'León, one of Venezuela's world-class salsa musicians who, at over 60-years-old and having featured on more than 50 albums, is still going strong — not bad for someone who only turned to music because he was fired from his job as a school-bus driver... after crashing the bus.

The man listening to the salsa is middle-aged. He says his name is Eduardo and he teaches guitar. I ask him about the Circo.

"It's a place for music, feeling and resistance," he explains, citing a government-type motto: "La música, la sensibilidad, la resistencia."

Resistance? To what?

"Well, we get threats from opposition politicians who say we are here illegally and from people who want the bullring returned to its original use, but we resist this exploitation. That's why the bulls won't return to the building to be exploited and killed, just like the capitalism that exploits artists won't return here to exploit us. Our success depends on our strength, our solidarity, our wish to fight."

What about music?

He gestures to the radio.

"You like? I like it. We are from different worlds. Music and song break down distances. It's not just for or from the student, the farmer, or the intellectual. Songs are part of being human; we are all human. We in the Circo take the music to the barrios, help the children see a world of music and opportunity."

He ends by singing a couple of lines: "Sequemos el sudor de nuestra frente y busquemos tras las nubes al sol busquemos con alborozo, el sol maravilloso de la revolución" ("We dry the sweat from our brows and seek, after the clouds, the sun, we seek with joy, the marvellous sun of revolution").

The lyrics are from 'Basta de Hipocresía' ('Enough Hypocrisy'), a song by Alí Primera. Primera was a popular Venezuelan folk, one-man-

147

and-a-guitar singer. To give an idea of his politically iconic status, in the poorer neighbourhoods, his features — slightly chubby and Jesus-like — appear graffitied alongside the heavyweights of Guevara and Castro. His 14 albums sing about the suffering of people destroyed by poverty and social inequality. Known as 'The People's Singer', Primera died in a car crash in 1985; twenty years later Chávez declared his music a 'national heritage'.

Primera's themes — equality, resistance, revolution, anti-capitalism, anti-exploitation, liberation — have become the staple repertoire of pro-Process bands. Often formed by groups from the barrios, these musicians are provided with places to practise (like Nuevo Circo), grants to record, coverage on government TV and gigs at pro-Chávez rallies. A cynic might be puzzled by their anti-capitalist rhetoric coming from a city where designer labels and Big Macs remain as popular as in any other, and wonder whether, despite their anti-exploitation rhetoric, these bands are aware that the government is, in a sense, exploiting them as a form of propaganda. The artists themselves, however, are adamant that they are conveying the message they want to express, so how can that be exploitation? Whatever your perspective, one thing is clear: in a country where music has long had a prominent role in everyday life, the Chávez government recognises and uses music's power.

During a recent public vote on a constitutional amendment, the government gave away free CDs marked "your right to copy is authorised". Each CD had 20 pro-government songs referring to "democracy and liberty", "going forth with Chávez" and "the death of capitalism and Uncle Sam". The first track, by Grupo Madera, is perhaps the most famous. A seven-piece from the Caracas slums, Grupo Madera used to create their own instruments from rubbish bins, but their catchy pro-Chávez tunes like, 'Uh! Ah! Chávez con su Pueblo Sí Va' ('Uh! Ah! Chávez *is* going forward with his people') with lyrics like "Children of the mother country, have confidence in the future... we will live in a Venezuela full of happiness" laid over salsa rhythms, has seen them shoot to stardom and their song become a *Chavismo* anthem. Other pro-Chávez bands to note (which support the Nuevo Circo collective) are two ska groups. One, PalmeraS KAnibales (Cannibal Palm Trees) was formed 17 years ago. They sound like ska crossed with the Chili Peppers and often feature a layered vocal sound reminiscent of a chorus of *mariachis*. Another, Dame Pa'Matala (Give Me Something To Kill It) fuses rap, ska, salsa and traditional Venezuelan instruments — flute, cuatro, and tambores — to produce a sound like politically conscious, acoustic rap.

These pro-Chávez bands aren't the kind that Ruben feeds into his car stereo as we cruise around Caracas. While the music he prefers avoids reference to revolution, it includes a vast range of styles: from Sentimiento Muerto (conventional but popular eighties Venezuelan rock), to Gaêlica (an amazing live band which combines Irish music and instruments with Latino beats); from C4 Trio (three *cuatro* players who produce impressive instrumental pieces), to Porn-O-Joint (one of the most baffling combinations of music styles, with each song swinging from reggae to hardcore, from rock to salsa) and Cabezón Key (Radiohead-esque rock).

Although opponents to the current administration claim that music's criticism of social issues is stifled, it's not strictly true. Founded in 1985, Desorden Público are probably Latin America's longest-running and most successful ska band — albeit ska mixed with the influence of jazz, big band, Latin beats and instruments. One of the most important contemporary groups in Venezuela, and politically veering towards the Chávez-like left, they are not afraid of giving a less-than-optimistic view of their country and its future. "The city is locked in to watch soap operas," they sing in 'Valle de Balas' ('Valley of Bullets'), "outside the guns don't respect, lead bursts but no one is alarmed."

In one sense, what Desorden Público notes is true. In parts of Caracas, murder is an everyday occurrence. In other areas the rich, driven to paranoia, spend much of their time locked inside multi-storey birdcages watching American TV, surrounded by electrified fences, armed guards and more barbed-wire than the Western Front. Meanwhile barrios sprawl nearby. There, given hope by The Process and direct aid from the missions, millions of urban migrants eke out an existence. The friction between these co-existing worlds creates something unique, disturbing and/or surprising. Turning a corner can mean the difference between a gilt-edged bubble and a world of guns and drugs. When these spheres collide, the effect, more often than not, is bone-shattering.

When I met a girl at a salsa club in a poor part of the city and took her back to my flat in a 'safe' zone for 'rich' ex-pats, I didn't expect to nearly die. It was 4am. She was a barrio girl pouring drinks. I went to the bathroom. When I came out, she was waiting, glass in hand. "*Tomala*," she said, pressing it to my lips. "Drink it." I glimpsed a creamy liquid. It wasn't the rum I'd seen her pouring. I took one mouthful and tasted flowers. Salsa still beating in my ears, I fell towards her.

It was still dark when I woke. My room had been ransacked. All my capitalist things of value had been liberated: passport, credit cards, laptop, camera, even the watch off my wrist. I ran downstairs, convinced that she must have just left — perhaps I'd been woken by the door closing. There was no sign of the girl. Feeling drunk, I banged on my neighbour's door, told them what had happened, contacted the embassy and realised it was 17 hours since the girl had spiked me. The police arrived. Big men with guns, they drove me to the local precinct and took my statement. A shaken-looking young man was also there. He had been held at gunpoint for eight hours in the back of his car while the men with guns went through the contacts on his mobile phone finding someone willing to pay a ransom. It's called 'express kidnapping'. I'd been lucky — £2,000 worth of stuff in exchange for my life. A bargain.

At dawn, we leave the Babylon Motorhome gig. Although a collective with links to the barrios and supporters of The Process, they played at a basement bar bursting with rich, young *caraqueños*. The rich invariably oppose the government and its ideologies, but, on this occasion, as long as the music played, political affiliation took a back seat. It doesn't matter where the musicians are from or what their political stance is. What matters is their music, and tonight that meant an ambient weave of electro, dub and salsa; bursts of trombone, accordion, sax and their singer's ethereal vocals.

Their singer, Elodie Bernardeau, is a French actress/musician who came to Caracas two years ago. She fell in love with the intense Venezuelan musical culture, wanted to contribute to the socialist process... and stayed. When not performing, she teaches drama to children in one of the barrios.

"Nothing is strange here," she explains to me, "but things surprise me every minute: most of all the musicians... their incredible feeling and talent, enthusiasm, generosity and versatility."

She may well be right, for as we drive away, through the city, we pass vast silent malls and hoardings advertising designer perfumes while on the pavements the homeless lie under cardboard blankets. Barrio men trundle old machines into the streets, ready to squeeze fresh orange juice for early-morning workers. And everywhere, in the distance, glimpsed between the glass canyons of multi-storey monoliths, are hillsides lost beneath barrios. It strikes me that, if nothing else, whether propagandist, modern, traditional, or any of the unique cocktails of instruments and styles occurring at this time in this country, Venezuelan musicians are special in their ability to let their art span and embrace the influences of these very different worlds.

HUNTING FOR DOGS

Think scoring an interview with Snoop is a hard job? You should try persuading Dog, a mechanic from Netherfield, to talk.

By Daddy Bones

From issue 2, Spring 2005

Break out a fresh pair of panties, bitches of Nottingham — Snoop Dogg is coming to town. He's the mack you can't help but love, and it's been over a decade since his last visit to Britain. *The Stool Pigeon* naturally wanted to grab an interview, so I started by calling his record label. "Snoop isn't talking to anyone on this tour," they say. What? Surely sometime in his week here there'll be a half hour when I might be allowed to hang off his shirt-tails while he pads about his hotel room crossing the 't's on an upcoming Hollywood movie deal or dotting the 'i's on the prototype for his upcoming signature barbecue unit, the Snoop DeGrill. The guy's an icon. Half the young western world is saying "fo' shizzle" because of him. He must be keen to explain himself to his British fans.

Four more calls later and it seems Snoop really is refusing to be interviewed. Pity. It might have been eventful, considering my record of needlessly disrespectful encounters with bona fide celebrities.

To John Cleese, between takes on a movie set: "Say John, can I get an auto... whoah, fuck ME you're tall, CAN YOU HEAR ME UP THERE?"

To Boy George at the adjacent urinal in a nightclub toilet: "Karma karma karma, are you trying to look at my cock?"

To Roy Walker in a refectory: "Fuck, sorry, was that your plate? SAY WHAT YOU SEE ROY! SAY WHAT YOU SEE! YOUR PASTA IS ON THE FLOOR!"

I wonder how the bad-boy megastar that has endured a public lifetime of murder trials and death threats would put up with my, uh, 'hard-line' questioning: "So, you're called Snoop 'cos your folks thought you looked like Snoopy the fat cartoon dog, yeah? Were they fucking blind or what? Snoopy was white, and to be frank, you look like a scrawny cat, if anything..."

I can see the eyes narrowing already.

"Your real first names are Calvin Cordozar, right? And you went and called your kids Corde, Cordell and Cori? Does your knowledge of the alphabet only go up to C? Honestly, not even Coco the Clown would be that stupid."

Oh well. Perhaps it's a good thing that Snoop is refusing to meet — he'd probably bust a cap in my ass if I let him know in person what I thought of his hair, all done up in those schoolgirl bunches. I did make an effort, though. I pestered the show's promoter. "No way," she kept telling me. "He won't even be at his own after-show party."

"Ignore her," said Stool Pigeon, "get into the show armed with a dictaphone and hunt him down. Pay off his bodyguards if you have to. Do whatever it takes. I'll reimburse you."

In Nottingham it's claimed that there are only ever a couple of degrees of separation between you and any other individual, and it's as untrue as the legend that there are five women to every man here, but to this end I secured myself what I thought was a dead-cert slot in the hottest spot of the Nottingham Arena. One of the fancy private viewing boxes there belongs to a local construction magnate who just so happens to be a good friend of my hizzo's pops. A few persuasive words later and I was sorted — not to hang about among the great unwashed, you understand — I was going to be in the best seat in the house, looking *down* on the motherfuckers. While ranks of council-estate neds threw spazzy gang signs in the stalls below, I'd be up in the gods, coolin' out in the icy glow of their countless phone LCD screens, sipping waitress-served gin & juice and getting a hustle on with the city's loftiest Havana-chompers.

If only someone had actually told them. If only someone had told *me* that they hadn't been told. I discover via text message just two hours before doors that my chain of nepotism had a weak link. My lady wasn't in town, her dad wasn't even in the country and I hadn't got a fucking ticket, had I? I couldn't even bring myself to call the editor and tell him I wasn't in. Instead I sulked — for hours. Finally, not wanting to throw an entire Saturday night down the pan, I accept an offer to join a few friends celebrating a birthday on trawl through some low-rent bars. I find temporary solace in a poisonous rotation of drinks — pear cider (a new one on me, never again), gin, beer, bourbon — whatever it takes to try and forget that right at this moment Snoop's band are busting out a classic and I ain't there to hear it.

Unwilling to endure a club when the pubs kick out, we wind up in an after-hours student bar so awful that people here wince when you mention its name. There is a collage of photographs on one of the bare brick walls depicting all manner of 'hilarity' previously witnessed within its confines — undergrads in underpants and ruddy-faced rugger lads (about to shit in a pint glass no doubt)... that kind of thing. Beside me at the bar is a fat lass in a skin-tight lime-green lamé catsuit. Her friend is dressed as Snow White, but she has the bodice on the wrong way round so it looks like she has tits protruding from her back.

As part of a futile attempt to bring joy to the remainder of the night, we plump for a large jug of some comically-named cocktail. Bizarrely, we find it contains just three shots of vodka and a glassful of sparkling wine — the remainder is dilute pink grapefruit squash. The draught lager tastes worse — it's flat and packs a metallic tang like the one you experience when licking the contacts on a nine-volt battery. We drink it anyway, slumped miserably on a torn, sticky sofa opposite the DJ booth. My head swims around the notion that things couldn't be more sour right now. And then the DJ fades out an Eminem joint, indulges a pregnant pause and plays Snoop's 'Drop It Like It's Hot'. The cunt. I swear he was laughing at me. Drunk and supremely pissed off I get up, put my jacket on and walk out — straight into the worst weather Nottingham has seen in recent memory.

With the wind taking branches off trees and whipping rain in sheets, all the cabs in the city are occupied, so I stagger home — uphill, into a howling headwind loaded with wet misery — while Snoop is no doubt cruising to a fine hotel in a warm limo. In fact, just then would have been the perfect time for his limo to swish right by me, veering into a huge puddle to soak me head-to-toe with filthy gutter-water. I finally fall through my front door looking like a shipwreck survivor, forego any preventative medicine for the oncoming hangover (a pint of water or a bite to eat maybe) and slug a throat-full of neat vodka from the fridge, crawl up the stairs and pass out. Somewhere, that fucking Snoop Dogg is grinning slyly. He's pleasantly stoned, lying on fresh sheets between two coffee-coloured bitches feeding him redcurrants and pink champagne, one nuzzling his ear with her glossy lips, the other tickling his nuts with her scarlet nails. I'm forced to settle for making it through the night alone without choking on my tongue.

When I come to and am able to move again, the following afternoon, I can only just make out the messages awaiting me. One is a guilt-inducing plea from the editor, along the lines of "tell me you made it in and it all went okay". The other is from my brother, somehow already informed that it went anything but. "Never mind, mate," he jokes, "you could always interview Dog."

Ah yes, of course — Dog, our trusty mechanic friend from Netherfield. Real name Dave, he acquired the charming title of 'Dog Bastard' following some comical misdemeanour that happened long before I met him. Now everyone in town just knows him as 'Dog'. In fact, when you call the garage he works at (and it's a right posh franchised one) even the customer service staff go blank if you ask for him by his real name. Good ol' Dog. This could turn out all smiles if I write it up well. I'll interview Dog for a laugh, turn the whole thing around, play on the name, make light of the missed opportunities and all that. I'll call him Monday.

"I don't get it, mate," he says on Monday.

"It's just a joke, Dog. I missed the Snoop show, so I'm gonna make it into a comedy thing where I interview you instead. You know, same name and all that..."

"I don't know nothin' about rap music, though. Some of it's alright, but I don't like none of that Indian stuff — nyeow nyeow nyeow..."

"Don't worry about it, it's not supposed to be serious — we can just make something up if you want. I want a picture of you, though. We can run it with one of Snoop and..."

"Whoa there! Yer fookin' jokin', right? There's no way you're gonna print a picture of me in a newspaper."

"Come on Dog, it'll be a laugh."

There's a pause. "Bones, mate, this bloke's back for his motor and I'm not done on it. Gizza ring later in the week."

Click.

And he hasn't answered the fucking phone since. So, I failed to bring you a scoop on the D O Double Gizzle and I couldn't even get a Q&A with my mate Dog, a Land Rover mechanic from Netherfield. Consider this my resignation, effective immediately.

CLOUD CANINE

Snoop Dogg loves his kids, never does the dishes, and we all need 'the white-wig-wearin' parliament motherfuckers' to let him back into Britain.

By Daddy Bones

From issue 24, December 2009

At long motherfucking lizzle. Twenty-two issues ago, in 2005, when *The Stool Pigeon* was just still hatching from its egg, we summarily failed to interview Snoop Dogg and it was galling to not get the chance to grab even a soundbite on that particular UK tour.

Finally, on the eve of his 10th solo album release, *Malice N Wonderland*, the now well-plumed *Pigeon* was offered a rare phoner with perhaps the best-loved and most famous black entertainer in the world. Twenty minutes on a low-volume, patched phone line to New York isn't quite the shining opportunity we'd hoped for, but even a long-distance yarn while his tour bus warms up is quite a kick. I mean, this is *Snoop Dogg* here. Who, aside from the British government that, in 2007, banned him from re-entering the UK following an entourage altercation at Heathrow, *doesn't* love Snoop Dogg?

Snoop is the bomb: the smooth operator who made West Coast hip hop a household sound; who changed the way the genre feels; and who can move into any field to which he takes fancy — cinema, TV, sports, porno — and come off with yet further respect and accolades. Few can do this and, in such respects, he *is* hip hop — or at least the embodiment of its expansive possibilities. Thirty million albums sold is a bullet-point, sure, and so is appearing as a judicial head-in-a-jar on *Futurama*, but I can think of no finer measure of his stature than that he was name-checked in *Father Ted*. Don't laugh. When an Irish writer needs the name of a rap figure to contextualise a line in his script, he picks the only one that everybody knows.

Yet it's only fairly recently, in this era of celeb-prodding media, have we really got to know what's behind the enduring image of the slang-talking pimp, crip walking from a haze of weed smoke. The documentary TV show, *Snoop Dogg's Father Hood*, showed Mister C.C. Broadus as the fun-loving family man, and his cameo in Sacha Baron Cohen's outrageous *Brüno* movie told us he was sharp enough to be in on a very blunt joke. Successful, stoned, sly *and* funny? Mother-*fucker*.

THE STOOL PIGEON: How are you, Snoop?
SNOOP DOGG: Higher than a motherfucker. Did a show last night with Method Man and Redman in Times Square.

SP: Three of the biggest stoners in America? All on one bill? Who were the roadies, Cheech & Chong?
SD: Yeah. Real talk.

SP: Do you still get a big kick out of playing live?
SD: Yeah, it's still the highlight for me; in front of a crowd, a live audience. Gives people a chance to be part of the music that they love.

SP: So with all these things you do in your life these days it's still...
SD: Yeah, 'cause there's still people who never seen me before. When I'm on-stage it gives them a chance to be part of something they been down with for a long time.

SP: Even though you've been doing this for 17 years, there's always a fresh generation...
SD: [Mishearing] Well, I think I'm the *second* generation. I think we on the fourth generation of rappers, but I'm like the second generation of rappers.

SP: Is this a big tour?
SD: This is just to promote my album: me, Devin the Dude, Redman and Method Man — just gettin' out and lettin' the people know that it's ready to come.

SP: It's not out in the States yet?

SD: Nah, December 8th.

SP: Christmas presents for the kids, right?

SD: Mmm-hm. Ex-*actly*.

SP: Is making music still as important to you as ever? I mean, you're pretty prolific...

SD: It's still one of the most important things in my life, 'cause that's what I'm dictated by — my music. I can do TV shows, movies and videos, but my life is essentially controlled by the music I make. It's my number one inspiration in life.

SP: When you were a kid, you were big into college football. You can't conceive the future, but...

SD: Nah, I thought I was gonna be playing basketball or football, know what I'm sayin'? As a kid, that's what my vision was, 'cause I was into sports and being athletic and just being on top of my game, you know? I was so *competitive*. I thought I would make it in that world before entertainment, and if I *did* make it in the entertainment world I was thinking of being a comedian. I was more of a funny guy.

SP: So even with all these strings to your bow, you think you might break off one day and be a stand-up comedian?

SD: Well, I do a bit of that. If you listen to my records, gotta lot of comedy in it; the movies I been in... I've always been able to put a little comedy in everything I do, because that's a part of me.

SP: Speaking of funny things, I swung by a second-hand record store today and saw something I haven't seen in a long time: a Tim Dog 12"...

SD: 'Fuck Compton'? They had that Tim Dog 'Fuck Compton' up in there?

SP: No, the follow-up: 'Bitch With A Perm' [possibly the meanest, most personal dis record ever]. Did you ever make peace with Tim Dog?

SD: I never even met that nigga! Oh, we killed his ass off *quick*! We went so hard on that nigga on the first tour, he was *gawn* after that! Nobody even cared about the nigga.

SP: You had the last laugh.

SD: Yeah, and I never met him. And I still go to New York all day, every day, so he must not been as gangsta as he said he was.

SP: New York rappers are still reticent to work with rappers from the West Coast and the South. Why is that?

SD: I think the rap game is just changing direction like it's supposed to. It moved off over to the west, the Midwest, and now it's down south. That's what it's supposed to do — go off. It's in Europe, it's in Japan, Asia, Africa... You gotta appreciate it for what it is; something that will never die.

SP: And it's still more important to you than anything?

SD: My life.

SP: What is your life actually like? You're a huge rapper known across the world and all that, but you're married with three kids. How old are your kids?

SD: 15, 12 and 10.

SP: Are they gonna follow in your footsteps?

SD: No, they got they own shoes to walk in. They don't need to walk in my shoes.

SP: What do they want to do when they grow up?

SD: I... I don't know. They still kids, still livin', so I let them live their life. I don't question what they wanna be or what they wanna do; they at the age where they learnin' themselves, so...

SP: That's sweet.

SD: Well, I remember when I was that age — you really need space. So let 'em be kids and become who they gonna be.

SP: Kids are forced to grow up too quick these days, I think.

SD: Yeah, you don't wanna shape and mould your kids because you gonna shape and mould som'n that you don't want. Let them find out who *they* are and let them become the best at whatever they gonna be — even if it's a criminal, a preacher, a doctor, or whatever it is. Let them find out, as opposed to trying to make them be something that they're not.

SP: You've got a lot of relatives in the music game. Isn't Brandy one of your cousins?

SD: Yeah, Brandy and Warren, they're ma cuz.

SP: And Nate Dogg, too.

SD: Yeah. They go hard.

SP: How is Nate? I heard he was ill.

SD: He doin' alright. Doing a little bit better.

SP: Some kind of lung problem?

SD: It's kinda hard to explain, but he's doing alright, so y'all just keep praying for him and he'll be up out of it sooner or later.

SP: Did he just stop recording? He seems to have been gone for such a long time...

SD: Mmm-*hmm*. [Long pause] Well, it's delicate; I can't really speak on that, so that's why I can't answer you.

SP: Sure. I've been checking the new album and the production credits and all, and was a little surprised there was no Dre.

SD: Why you surprised? I made three albums without Dr Dre. He don't dictate my sound.

SP: I just thought he was due back with you. But you two are still best friends?

SD: We're *great* friends, but sometimes I like doin' shit on my own, man, where I don't have to become dependent on nobody.

SP: Do you do much production yourself?

SD: I *can*, but I mean... there's certain situations where I don't put myself in that position, 'cause I got people who are better at that than me. Every time I do a record, I go for a different look, a different sound, a different feel, conceptually. To get with Dr Dre, it's gotta be a concept thing. I don't just fuck with him on some once-in-a-lifetime; we gotta do some concepts. That's why everything we done is great and timeless. We don't just do it here or there; we come with great conceptual projects.

SP: Will you work with him fully again?

SD: I never stopped working with him. Just because you don't hear him on my album don't mean that I ain't working with him. I might work on one of his artists' projects or give him an idea, or he might mix one of my songs. It's more about just being down with each other. Sometimes you wanna create your own atmosphere. To me, Ice Cube is the best example: he sounded great when he was with Dre, but when he left Dre he created his own *sound*. To ever get back with Dre again, it'd be great, but you don't not listen to Cube 'cause he ain't got Dre, and that's the thing that I been doin' — creating my own sound, whether I'm working with Pharrell, Timbaland, The Dream or Teddy Riley. Whoever I'm working with, it's my sound, it ain't *they* sound.

SP: Is it just an American tour you're doing?

SD: Yeah, but I'm comin' to Europe, though, so don't trip. Y'all gonna get it sooner or later.

SP: You need to come back to Britain. We need to sort that out.

SD: Yeah, they need to let me in and quit bullshittin'! They acting like bitches over there! Let me in the motherfuckin' place!

162

SP: Who decided you can't come in, the Home Office?

SD: Well, the *people* — they want me there and love me and wanna see me. It's the motherfuckin' *government*. Some white-wig-wearin' *parliament* motherfuckers. They running they shit based on the 1800s, as opposed to the 2000s. Y'all livin' in *yesteryear*! Y'all need to change your shit over there!

SP: Okay, no politics — dull subject — but it makes me think of money, and you do have a lot of that. What do you do with your money?

SD: Well, you can't die with it! Fuck it! Spend that shit! What you gonna do? Save and shit? I like to spread it out: my investment is in the community and the people who wanna do something with themselves — and give *them* an opportunity.

SP: What kind of things? The school football team that you coach?

SD: I got a Little League football *league* that I started: The Snoop Youth Football League — a whole league that I been runnin' for five years. We had over 20,000 kids from the inner cities sign up and participate and play.

SP: Will it ever go national?

SD: It's only in California now, but it will continue to spread and *will* go outside of California next year. I invest a lot of my money and more of my *time* into that, because time is more important than money when you're dealing with trying to bring change, you know?

SP: It's great you got the opportunity to do this.

SD: Yeah, but my *money* don't mean as much as my time and devotion. Motherfuck a million dollars. I can give you a million dollars and say, 'Here man, I love you,' but if I can give you a million dollars' worth of game, you can go out, make *three* million, give me a million, and now *you* got two million. I'd rather teach you how to create your own way, as opposed to giving you something that don't give you no attitude to wanna work.

SP: Do you ever bring your family when you tour?

SD: No, they in school, and my wife's doing her business, so... this is like me going to work, or going to the armed forces. I go to war on my own, and I come back with the goods.

SP: I've seen the show *Father Hood*. That was a good show. It's so clearly obvious that you're a devoted father and husband, and you really have a lot of fun with the kids.

SD: Yeah, we're real partial. We're real close — not fake, and we're not Hollywood. We're more on the page of friends. I'm not even like their father — I'm like their *friend*. I wanna be like that, 'cause a friend they'll tell anything, but a father they'd hide certain things from. So that's our relationship.

SP: Do you find they have any issues because they're the sons and daughter of Snoop Dogg?

SD: They handle all *that* shit. They been dealing with it since they was born.

SP: They go to school in LA?

SD: Yeah. Catholic school; my eldest son is in high school.

SP: You sent them to a Catholic school?

SD: [Quietly] They mama did that. But realistically it was the best thing for 'em. I see my kids are some good kids for going to a Catholic school.

SP: Did you grow up with religion in your house?

SD: Yeah, we went to church every Sunday and Tuesday.

SP: Sunday *and* Tuesday!?

SD: It was like *Bible* study or som'n.

SP: A lot of rappers convert to Islam. Did you once join The Nation?

SD: I didn't *join* The Nation of Islam, I roll with 'em. Fruits of Islam, Nation of Islam... Mr Farrakhan is a personal friend of mine. I love and support everything that they do, so... that's what it is. There's only one god in the world. Regardless whether you Christian, Muslim, Baptist, whatever — no matter what your belief is — there's only one god you prayin' to. So I don't classify myself as a Muslim or Christian, I'm just a god-fearing person who loves god, loves life and that's how I *carry* my life. When I roll with the Jewish people, nobody say that I'm a black Jew, but when I roll with The Nation of Islam, y'all wanna say I'm a Muslim. I eat plenty bacon. Do plenty shit. And that's just what it is.

SP: I love bacon. You can't beat it.
SD: You really can't.

[EMI rep: Okay, one more question and Snoop's gotta get rollin'.]

SP: Damn, now I can't remember what the fuck I was gonna ask you.
SD: Take another sip of your drink, it'll come to you.

SP: Okay, everyone knows Snoop Dogg — he smokes weed, he's the pimp, and all that — but you're nearly 40, a family man and a real smart guy. Do you still feel the need to present a persona when you record?
SD: It was *never* a persona with me: it was me; it was my life. You gotta understand that a lot of rappers are not living a persona, they're living their lives. For real.

SP: I understand that, but...
SD: ...this shit is real. And, as you get older, that life that you live becomes either a homely life — you have a wife and kids — or it becomes real reckless and wild with you and your homies and *then* you have kids. You gotta understand, when most rappers come in the game, they don't have kids, wives, relationships... It's based on them, their

165

neighbourhoods, their homies and what they grew up about. So that's what they rap about: what the fuck they goin' through. When they get older, like myself, then you start to feel like a rapper has fell off, or went away from what you're normally accustomed to. But he's just growing as a man; as a person.

SP: So you don't feel like you should start rapping about doing the dishes and putting the kids to bed?

SD: I don't *never* do the dishes! So why would I rap about it? I got a motherfuckin' *maid* to do that shit!

SP: Let me ask about porn, because it's a subject close to my heart...

SD: Heh. You like porno, huh?

SP: Who doesn't?

SD: Well, that's why I made a few! I know everybody like it, but everybody be afraid and 'shamed, so I was like, 'Fuck it, I'm gonna put together a coupla porno movies. I'm gonna direct and add a different flavour to the porno world just to change the game.' And I did. I won four AVN awards, sold the most DVDs ever in porno, brought a new style of shooting, brought music to the porno world... I changed the whole game and they thankful for me. They want me to do more, but I'm like, 'I'm cool, that was a phase for me and I don't wanna do it no more.'

SP: You can't do that forever with a wife and kids, I suppose...

SD: I had a wife and kids when I did it! That didn't stop nothin'. I just didn't wanna do it no more.

SP: Anything you wanna do that you're yet to do?

SD: Yeah. I feel like a gotta win a motherfuckin' Grammy.

SP: More than an Oscar?

SD: Yeah, real shit. But I'ma get one of those, too.